STRANGE TALES OF SCOTLAND

by

Calum McLaren
Andrew Livingston
Gail MacFarlane
and
Lorraine Griffiths

Illustrated by John Mackay

"Strange Tales of Scotland", a compilation from the Lang Syne local series, was published by Lang Syne Publishers Ltd., Newtongrange, Midlothian, in 1980; re-issued in 1981, 1982, 1983, 1984, 1985, 1986, and this edition 1987, and printed by Waterside Printers, Old School, Blanefield, Glasgow.
© Lang Syne Publishers Ltd. 1980.
ISBN 0 0946 264 147

STRANGE TALES OF SCOTLAND

INTRODUCTION

How did a glowing hand assure King Robert the Bruce of victory at the Battle of Bannockburn? What happened to witches in olden times? Where did a castle laird rise from the grave? Who was murdered by a phantom hand? Why did a skeleton have to stand trial? How did a miracle in East Lothian lead to the foundation of Glasgow? Who was the hidden monster of Glamis Castle? Why did an earl's son give his shadow to the Devil? Who had three bodies?

These are just some of the questions answered in the dozens of stories which have been selected for this edition of "Strange Tales of Scotland."

You can also find out about: the odd green Ladies of Stirling and Edinburgh; the wolf who saved a town from destruction, hills where zombie knights ride their silent horses, the man boiled in lead by angry locals, the murder trial sparked off after allegations by a ghost, the Pitlochry bogle, the greedy blacksmith forced to swallow as much gold as he could carry, the lad who had to shoot an arrow at his mother, and the heartbroken girl who ordered her servants: "Bury me alive!"

We visit magic wells and look at some mysterious river spirits. The case of a minister who murdered his wife in the manse and then went next door to calmly preach Sunday morning service in church is examined. There is the legend of a king's encounter with a dangerous stag which apparently led to the foundation of Holyrood Abbey. We have the case of the two naughty monks burned alive. . .the man driven into the next world by ghostly hounds. . .and many more equally spine chilling tales.

BIBLIOGRAPHIC NOTE

"Strange Tales of Scotland" is a compilation of material published in the following Lang Syne titles:- Strange Tales of the Borders, Strange Tales of the Lothians, Strange Tales of Old Edinburgh, Strange Tales of North-East Scotland, Strange Tales of Tayside, Tales of St. Giles & Holyrood, Stirling and Trossachs Life in Days Gone By, and Ghosts, Smugglers & Secrets of Britain's Inns.

Coffins on Arthur's Seat

Five Edinburgh lads found more than they bargained for when they went hunting rabbits on Arthur's Seat one summer afternoon in 1836.

A dog they'd taken with them started scratching at the hillside. One of the boys went to investigate and found what looked like the entrance to a tiny cave.

He put his head inside to see what was there, and quickly withdrew it again. The hole was full of coffins!

There were seventeen of them, arranged in three tiers. Each one was four inches long and carved out of single pieces of wood, apart from the lids, which were fixed on with brass pins. The sides were decorated with minute tin designs.

The boys - unaware of the stir their find was to cause - immediately broke some of the coffins by throwing them at each other. But next day they gave the rest to their schoolmaster, who belonged to the local archaeological society.

Curious, he prised the lid off one of them, and was amazed to find a diminutive figure inside, carved in perfect detail. Further inspection showed that the other boxes had the same bizzare contents.

Soon Edinburgh was buzzing with the news of the boys' find. There were endless discussions about the origin of the coffins, and even the London 'Times' devoted half a column to the story.

Could it be that the macabre miniatures were designed to bring about the end of some witch's enemy? It is possible, but to this day the coffins - some of them are now in the National Museum of Antiquities in Queen Street - have kept the strange secret of their origin.

Angelical Thomas

Edinburgh's most infamous pair of Satanic malefactors were never actually convicted of witchcraft, yet their activities became firmly impressed on the minds of the city's ordinary folk as being connected with the Devil.

They were Major Thomas Weir and his sister Jean. Born in Carluke in 1599, Weir received his rank after active service in Ireland with Montrose's Covenanters. On his return to civilian life he became a captain in Edinburgh's City Guard, and it's said that he commanded the guard when Montrose was executed in 1650.

Weir remained a strict Covenanter, so he took up residence in the now demolished West Bow, which linked the Lawnmarket to the Grassmarket. There lived several members of a sect that suited his beliefs - the "Bowhead Saints."

They were a sanctimonious lot, who spent most of their time either praying or congratulating themselves and each other on their piety. They held meetings in their homes, and Weir became so important in the group that he was able to choose where he would pray. Only the houses of "Saints of the highest Form" were good enough for the Major.

He was certainly an impressive character. He was tall, and dark in complexion, and a contemporary writer tells of his "grim countenance". To complete the effect, he usually wore a dark cloak, and carried round with him a tall black staff, carved with the heads of fabulous creatures.

The women of the group called him "Angelical Thomas," so imposing was his appearance, and so fine his praying voice. The members asked for his advice on problems, and coveted his presence at meetings.

Weir continued in this happy situation until 1670, and then events took a turn that none of his flock could have anticipated in their wildest nightmares. Their cosy world was shattered when Thomas revealed that he had been leading a double life. The pious front he had presented to them for twenty-five years, reflecting all that they aspired to, was a sham.

It was a dramatic moment. The cream of the Bowhead Saints were in the Major's house, expecting to listen to him pray. Instead, they heard a minutely detailed catalogue of a lifetime of fornication, bestiality, and incest with his sister.

The congregation were appalled. They concluded that Weir must have taken leave of his senses, and concluded that he must be made a prisoner in his own home before his confessions became public and brought the whole group into disrepute.

Word was passed around that he was dangerously ill, and the cover-up worked well enough for a few months. But the shallowness of their religious zeal was to be their undoing.

The Reverend John Sinclair, a minister at Ormiston, was among those who heard Weir's story. He had always been envious of the Major's preaching ability, and decided to discredit him by telling the whole story to the Lord Provost, Sir Andrew Ramsay.

Ramsay's reaction was the same as the Saints'. He arranged for Weir to be examined by doctors to find if he was sane. They reported that he was - his only problem, they said, was a ravaged conscience. When clergymen made the same diagnosis, the Provost had no alternative but to order Weir and his sister in the Tollbooth.

If James was sane, it seems that the same could not be said for his sister. Though the charge against her was incest, she proceeded to shock her examiners with endless tales of communion with the Devil. She revealed the mark of a horse-shoe on her brow, and told how she and her brother had travelled to Musselburgh in a flaming coach to make an undertaking with Satan.

She explained that the Major's staff was an instrument of magical power. It was the source of the skills that the West Bow sect had found so irresistible, and allowed him to live his twilight life without discovery - for as long as his nerve held, at any rate.

Weir corroborated her story, and on 9 April, 1670, the pair appeared in the Justiciary Court. Charges of sorcery formed the bulk of the indictments faced by Jean, but her brother was mostly accused of debauchery of various sorts.

Surprisingly, considering the age in which they lived, they were acquitted on the charges of witchcraft. It was rare in those days for the magistrates to pass up the chance of doing away with anyone who professed the vaguest connection with the 'Muckle Deil.'

But they were found guilty on the other charges, and sentenced to death. 'Angelical Thomas' met his end at the Gallow Lee, an execution site near where the Playhouse Cinema now stands. He declined to make a final prayer for forgiveness. "Let me alone," he said. "I have lived as a beast, and I must die as a beast." He was duly strangled and burned at the stake.

Jean's last act as she stood before a huge crowd on the Grassmarket gallows was to try to remove her clothes! The executioner managed to salvage what little dignity there was in the situation, and she was hanged.

Predictably, the West Bow house that had once been a haven of godliness came to be regarded as haunted by spirits of a less holy kind. The Major's magic staff was reported to open the gateway to Hell, letting in strange spirits which danced till dawn. Weir himself was seen, galloping down the narrow streets on a fiery, headless horse. And occasionally passers-by reported seeing him arrive at his former home in the Devil's coach, drawn by six black chargers. The meetings of the Bowhead Saints were never quite the same again!

Death at Bruntsfield

One of the grimmest of Auld Reekie's ghost tales concerns the Wrychtishousis, an ancient mansion that stood at the edge of Bruntsfield Links on the site now occupied by James Gillespie's School.

In the middle of the 18th century it was occupied by General Robertson of Lawers, who was staying in Edinburgh while his Perthshire home underwent alterations.

On the first morning of his stay the general was amazed to find his servant in a state of abject terror. The man claimed he had been visited by ghosts - a headless woman had been pacing the floor, he said, carrying a young child.

Robertson abruptly dismissed the servant's story, and refused to let him move to another room. But the spectral visitations persisted, and by the time the household moved back to Perthshire the man was thin with worry, and in a poor state of health.

The incident was forgotten until some years after the General's death, when his niece received a visit from a friend at Lowes. The Wrychtishousis had been the home of this woman's family, and in the course of conversation she asked if anything strange had happened during Robertson's stay.

The servant was quickly summoned, and was only too glad to tell of his terrible experiences. A grim story then unfolded which gave awful substance to his tale.

Renovations to the house had revealed a hidden closet. Horrified workmen found in it a chest containing the skeletons of a woman and a baby. And worst of all, the box was too short to hold the woman's outstretched body - so her head had been cut off and laid by her corpse.

A confession written by the perpetrator of the deed was also found in the closet.

Many years before, the Wrychtishouses' owner had gone abroad to war, leaving his wife and child in the care of a younger brother. But the man died in battle - and the brother murdered his widow and son to gain ownership of the house.

One wonders if the servant would have slept any better at Bruntsfield if he'd known about the awful secret hidden in the wall near his bed!

In the Wizard's Lair

Not all of Edinburgh's spectres were as terrifying as the one that appeared in the Wrychtishouses.

Early last century a soldier named William Patullo moved with his wife into the house in the West Bow where Weir the Wizard had spent his infamous life of evil. The house had been boarded up since the Wizard's execution at the stake in 1670.

No-one had dared even to enter the place for fear of a dreadful fate, and the neighbourhood was alive with speculation about the terrors in store for Patullo.

Sure enough, as he and his wife lay in bed on their first night in the place, a wraith appeared - in the form of a calf! It stood at the end of the bed, then put its fore-feet on the mattress and gazed unblinking at them for some time before it vanished.

Their experience was a great disappointment to the gossips, who had expected more sensational events. But it was enough for the Patullos. They found quieter accommodation, and the Wizard's lair was once more closed up.

Morningside's Green Lady

It was a happy day for Sir Thomas Elphinstone when he visited his life-long friend, the Earl of Glencairn, in London. For he fell in love with the Earl's daughter, Betty, who was forty years his junior. Sir Thomas asked Glencairn for the girl's hand in marriage, and immediately received his friend's permission. But Betty was less than happy about the situation. She was in love with a dashing young officer, whom she knew by his regimental name of Captain Jack Courage.

Unfortunately, Jack had been posted to Ireland, and so the wedding went ahead. Elphinstone and his bride moved into his mansion, which still stands in Morningside, overlooking Craiglockhart and the Myreside playing fields. Now only one thing remained to make Sir Thomas' happiness complete - that Betty should meet his son, John, who was serving in the army.

Four months after the marriage John came home, and Betty discovered to her horror that her new step-son was none other than her lost love, Jack Courage. The situation was for him to leave the house. It was a sad and tender moment when the young couple said their farewells a few days later.

John begged a first and last kiss, and they embraced, only to be interrupted by Elphinstone coming into the room. As soon as he realised what was happening, the old man flew into an uncontrollable rage, and stabbed Betty through the heart with a dagger.

Immediately he broke into tears, and begged his son's forgiveness. John lifted the corpse, and laid it on the bed upstairs. The next morning, he returned to the room, to find his father kneeling beside the bed with his arms around his victim. He was dead.

They were buried together, but Betty's body was more easily laid to rest than her soul. John leased the mansion, and his tenants were horrified to see Betty appear before them, wearing the green dress in which she had died.

An oriental mystic was called in to communicate with her. She complained that her coffin was too close to Elphinstone's. A new vault was built, and some years later Jack Courage's coffin was placed beside that of his lover. The Green Lady was never seen again.

White Lady of Corstorphine

Walking along Dovecote Road in genteel Corstorphine, one would hardly expect to be confronted by the spectre of a White Lady, pacing her ghostly path in eternal torment. Nevertheless, several people have reported seeing her.

The innocent sycamore in one of the resident's gardens, and the circular, three-storey building that gives the street its name, testify to a grim and passionate scene that was enacted there nearly 400 years ago.

Christian Nimmo, wife of a prosperous Edinburgh merchant, was in love with James, Laird of Forrester. The sycamore was their meeting-place, and they spent many happy hours together there.

But Lord James had his faults - he was continually in debt, and spent too much time in the local taverns. One night, when he was the worse for drink, they quarrelled and he insulted Christian viciously. She brooded on his churlishness for a few days, then rushed to see him at his home, Corstorphine Castle.

It turned out that he was drinking again, so Christian sent her maid to fetch him from the Black Bull in the High Street. James was in a furious temper when he arrived at the sycamore. Instead of apologising, he renewed his attacks on her, and in her anger she pulled his sword from its scabbard and killed him.

Horrified by what she had done, Christian dashed to the Castle to hide, leaving her lover in a pool of blood. But she was soon found. There could be no doubt about the verdict at her trial, and she was sentenced to death.

She managed to have the execution delayed twice, and even escaped from the Tollbooth prison where she was imprisoned. But on 12 November, 1679, Christian Nimmo finally paid the price for her passionate deed, and was beheaded.

It is said that she can still be seen wandering near the sycamore, dressed in white and carrying a bloodied sword. Moreover, an awful curse hangs over the Dovecote - if it's demolished, says the legend, the lady of the house in whose grounds it stands will die within the year.

The Haunted Attic

About a century ago a street of tall, dark houses occupied a site now filled by new flats, near the Botanical Gardens. Neighbours were full of gossip about a man who lived in one of them. Good looking and well-to-do, he rarely left his home, and never received visitors.

Eventually he died. The house was locked up, and lay vacant for many years. Residents on either side claimed they could hear stange voices coming from it, but they soon stopped, and most people forgot about them.

Then, at the beginning of the First World War, an Englishman took over the property, and opened it as a boarding house. Its peeling paint-work was renewed, and the rooms were let - except the attic, from which voices were heard once more.

One day, when business was going particularly well, and all the other rooms were full, the landlord rented the garret to a young couple. They, too, heard someone talking inside, and rang for the house-keeper. The unfortunate woman opened the door and walked in, then let out a piercing scream.

The couple found her standing by a bed, gazing upwards. She was speechless with terror, and remained so for the rest of her life. There was a presence in that attic more dreadful than her sanity could cope with!

The story reached the University, and a Divinity student named Andrew Muir decided to find out for himself what was happening. He arranged with the landlord to go into the room with two bells. He would ring one if he saw something, and the other if he needed help.

He entered the attic at ten o'clock one evening. A few moments later the landlord heard both bells ring, and dashed into the room. Andrew Muir was sitting at a table, with a look of inexpressible horror on his face. He had died instantaneously of sheer terror. The house was locked up again, and the awful room never saw the light of day again, until the demolisher's hammer erased its secret for ever.

Robert Weir

Murder at midnight put a brutal end to the life of John Kincaid, Laird of Warriston, one July night in 1600. It was four years before his killer came to justice, but his wife, who had engineered the crime, was brought to book more quickly.

Lady Warriston - born Jean Livingston, daughter of the Laird of Dunipace - harboured a passionate loathing of her husband. No record of her trial has survived, so the cause of her hatred died with her. Rumour has it that Kincaid was a brutal man. Theirs may have been a marriage of convenience between two influential families. On the other hand, Jean may have been in love with someone else, for she gave birth to a child shortly before the murder, and according to a contemporary ballad the Laird claimed it was not his.

Whatever the reason, Lady Warriston contacted Robert Weir, one of her father's servants, and told him that she could not bear to live with her husband any longer. Weir agreed to help her and on the evening of July 1 she hid him in a cellar at Warriston house. At twelve o'clock he crept upstairs to Kincaid's room and, with Jean watching, struck him a heavy blow.

If it had been effective, the plot might never have been discovered. But Weir had been clumsy - the Laird woke up and started to fight back. They struggled for some time, as Weir tried to throttle his victim, and Kincaid screamed for help. But soon the master of the house was dead, and Lady Warriston sat in the hall in a state of shock, horrified at what she had done.

Weir fled the city, promising Jean that if the murder was discovered he would not betray her. It was a noble gesture, but unnecessary. The truth came out quickly, and the Magistrates were just as swift to order her execution. She was hanged within a few days, and in June, 1604, Robert Weir paid a terrible price for his part in the crime. The idea of a servant killing a Laird was outrageous, and he was sentenced to be broken on the wheel.

Nicol Muschet

September 5, 1719, was an unlucky day for Margaret Hall. It was the date of her marriage to Nicol Muschet - outwardly a promising young medical man, but in fact a callous good-for-nothing who was to send his bride to her grave just over a year later.

Muschet learned early in life the pleasures available in Edinburgh at the turn of the century. Nevertheless, he trained as a medical student, and after a brief apprenticeship to a surgeon in Alloa he returned to the capital to work as an apothecary's assistant.

Then he met Margaret. Muschet claimed later that pressure from his friends and the girl forced him into marriage. Whatever the reason, they were wed - but only two months later he was planning to leave his estate in the hands of an administrator and desert her.

The plan fell through after complications and Nicol had to find another way out. Then he met James Campbell of Burnbank - whom he described in his confessions as "the only Vice-regent of the Devil." But he was happy enough to act on Campbell's suggestions for getting rid of Margaret.

He paid a friend of Burnbank £50 to lure her into a compromising situation, so that a fraudulent divorce could be obtained. When this failed, he embarked on a fantastic series of bids to murder the girl. First he tried poisoning her with mercury. She spent weeks in agony, but recovered. Then he hired footpads to kill her in a close. Despite several attempts - which Margaret evaded by sheer luck - this ploy also failed.

Eventually Muschet decided to do the deed himself. It seems incredible that she still harboured any love or trust for her husband, but she offered no objection when he asked her to go to Duddingstor with him through the King's Park late at night on 17 October, 1720.

At the last moment she realised what he intended, but it was too late. murdered her, and left her lying on Duke's Walk. But his last atte was as clumsy as the others, for he left a sleeve at the scene of the cr Muschet ended his miserable life at the end of the hangman's r

Eugene Chantrelle

A similar case to that of Nicol Muschet happened over a century later. The victim this time was Elizabeth Dyer, who at the age of fifteen, fell in love with her French teacher at Newington Academy. Eugene Chantrelle was certainly a romantic figure. Born in Nantes in 1834, he was a distinguished student at the city's medical school, and looked forward to a successful career. His father died when the boy was fifteen, however, and he had to leave school to support himself.

From then on Chantrelle became a drifter, unable to fulfill his early potential. He fled France for political reasons, and lived in America for some time. Then, after four years in England, he came to teach in Edinburgh.ı. A handsome charmer with an air of cynicism, it is understandable that the young girl found him attractive.

Unfortunately, Eugene responded to her infatuation. Within a few months she became pregnant, and at sixteen she was married to Chantrelle in order to save her reputation. Before long, she was to pay for her good name with her life.

They moved into a house at 81 George Street, and almost immediately Chantrelle's anger at the situation in which he found himself began to show. He beat Elizabeth continually, and spent as much time as he could away from home in the city's taverns. In 1876 he appeared in court, charged with assaulting a servant and threatening his wife.

Elizabeth's position became increasingly desparate, but she refused to leave for fear that publicity in the divorce court might harm her three children. But by 1877 Chantrelle had given up teaching, and was in considerable debt. That October, he insured Elizabeth's life for £1000 against accidental death.

On New Year's Day, of the next year, she became ill, and shortly afterwards she died in the Royal Infirmary. Chantrelle claimed that a gas leak had killed her. But the police had their own ideas about the cause of Elizabeth's death.

A doctor diagnosed narcotic poisoning, and traces of opium were found on the girl's nightdress. A quantity of the drug was found in Chantrelle's room, and his gas story collapsed when a long disused pipe was found. It had been deliberately fractured.

Chantrelle was found guilty of murder after a four day trial, and hanged.

William Bennison

Religious hypocrisy was never far beneath the surface of Edinburgh life, but the case of William Bennison is one of the worst of false piety.

Born in Ireland, he married an Irish girl, Mary Mullen, in 1838. Soon afterwards he left her, and bigamously married Jean Hamilton, of Paisley. Then he returned to Mary, and asked her to come to Scotland with him. When they arrived, she died mysteriously , and was buried in an unmarked grave.

He went back to Jean, and they moved into a house near Leith Walk. They had a daughter, and lived happily enough for several years. Both had strong religious convictions, and they became enthusiastic and hard-working Methodists.

But Bennison's attendance at prayer meetings took a distinctly unspiritual turn. He began to see a girl called Margaret Robertson, and soon afterwards told friends that his wife was in bad health. In fact she was perfectly well - but not for long. In February 1850 he bought some arsenic from an apothecary, and within a fortnight Jean was painfully ill. The ghoulish Bennison declared to her sister when asked for a doctor: "it is no use, she is going home to glory."

He took a pair of black trousers to be mended, saying he would need them if his wife died, and later the same day she did. Bennison promptly took the wedding ring from her finger, and moved in with Margaret Robertson's family.

But his sister-in-law was suspicious, first when he refused to allow a post-mortem, and then when a neighbour's dog died after eating the remains of the food he had used to poison Jean.

There was nothing the police could use as evidence, however, but the murderer's arrogance betrayed him in the end. He went to the apothecary from whom he had bought the arsenic, admitted he had used it to kill his wife, and asked the incredulous chemist to do him a service by not mentioning it to anyone!

Justice soon caught up with William Bennison, and he was hanged. But not before he had stood in the dock and called on Heaven to forgive the Crown witnesses!

William Sinclair

Student sit-ins are often thought of as an unfortunate symptom of our times, but few people know that they hold a time-honoured place in Edinburgh tradition!

One of the main centres of such activity was the Royal High School. "Barring out" of masters took place several times during the late 16th century, usually in support of claims for an extra holiday.

The pupils would gather a store of food and arms, then lock the school doors. Usually the buildings had to be taken by storm, and then there were fines to be paid and painful punishments to be received. Occasionally boys were jailed, and sometimes holidays were reduced instead of extended.

On 15 September, 1595, there was another "barring out," the start of an affair that would eventually involve the King himself. The school's quaintly-named Rector, Hercules Rollock, was first to arrive on the scene.

He was met by barricades, and a demand for a holiday. He reasoned with the boys, then threatened them, but they would not budge. Eventually he gave up, and asked the Magistrates to help.

Soon a group of city officers arrived, led by Baillie John McMorane. He also tried to persuade the boys to leave. When they refused, he ordered his men to break down the door with a battering ram.

The pupils shouted dreadful threats as the door began to give way. The Baillie would receive "a pair of bullets through his head," according to one boy. Sure enough, a few moments later one of the ring-leaders, William Sinclair, aimed a pistol through a window, and shot McMorane in the head.

His men were dumbfounded, but soon Sinclair and seven of his colleagues were in the Tollbooth The Town Council convened, and sent a message to King James VI.

James decided that since the boys belonged to noble and powerful families, it would be against his interests for any action to be taken against them. They went to trial, but were acquitted on James' orders - because they were all under fourteen years of age!

June Snowball

Bring me a snowball in June and you can live rent free for a year! That was the strange request made by the Duke of Lauderdale in the 17th century when Thomas and Margaret Hardie, tenants of his farm at Lauder, confessed they'd no money with which to pay the annual rent.

So the first time snow fell Maggie made a giant ball and hid it in a cave at their farm which was called Tollishill. She built stones around it and inspected the ball each day. I'm not quite sure what she did. All I do know is that the snowball didn't melt and the Duke, noted as a tough landlord, kept his side of the bargain.

Later when he was locked up in a London prison for life as one of the captives from the Battle of Worcester Maggie was able to do him a good turn.

In the years following the battle the farm became very successful and she saved a lot of gold coins. Eventually a giant bannock was baked, with the money inside, and off Maggie went with it to London singing all the way.

She eventually got into Lauderdale's cell and gave him the bannock. Inside he found enough gold coins to pay for his freedom.

In 1660, when he got home, the Duke gifted her with a silver girdle as a reward. This was handed down through the generations and presented to the Scottish National Museum of Antiquities at the turn of the century.

Hangman's Perk

Many folk departed this life on the end of a hangman's rope at Dumfries particularly during the years between 1479 and 1722 when the persecution of so-called witches was carried out with appalling ferocity.

The hangman in Scottish towns was always well paid but in Dumfries one of his perks led to a court action.

Every market day he had the right to walk through the town with a large spoon and take as much meal or corn as it would carry from the sacks on display.

Eventually the farmers got fed-up with this costly practice and went to law. But the court came out in the hangman's favour. They said it was his right.

Many farmers hit back by boycotting the market and taking their hard won products elsewhere.

Back from the Dead

The case of a shopkeeper who vanished after receiving an order from A CORPSE for a pair of shoes still has Selkirk baffled to this day.

At the centre of the riddle was Rabbie Heckspeckle - busy shoemaker and nosey parker extraordinary. Nothing happened in town without him knowing about it. And he could've written a book on the lives of local inhabitants which perhaps explains why he was so intrigued by a stranger who called at the shop one morning and asked for a pair of shoes.

While taking measurements Rabbie fired questions galore to find out who the customer was and where he'd come from but all to no avail.

"Ah'll be back the morn - same time. Hae the shoes ready then," said the customer.

All that day our shoemaker quizzed other callers at the shop about "Mr X." He felt a bit uneasy when told that his description of the customer resembled a man from a parish some distance away who had recently died.

Sure enough the fellow was back next morning, paid for the shoes, and left. But Rabbie was on his trail. He had to know just exactly who this chap was!

Minutes later poor Heckspeckle was shaking like a leaf as he watched "Mr X" go into the graveyard, lie down in front of a tombstone and vanish.

He fled back to town and burst into the nearest public place to spout out his tale. Soon it was round every house and business. . .Selkirk was in uproar.

Civic chiefs decided to open the grave and there the corpse was found complete with one pair of brand new shoes.

Fearing some kind of dark disturbance our superstitious forefathers had a new coffin made and re-interred the body.

But being practical at the same time Rabbie concluded that the shoes wouldn't be much use to their owner so he took them back to the shop and the most novel bargain of the century went on sale.

However it seems that was a bad mistake. Later he vanished. Again that grave was opened. Inside lay the corpse with the shoes. In its hands was: Rabbie's nightcap. . .

The Wraith in Room Three

The Cross Keys Hotel, Peebles, is reputedly haunted by the ghost of Marion Ritchie who was its first landlady back in the 18th century.

In her day Marion, who was immortalised by Sir Walter Scott as Megg Dodds in St. Ronans Well, kept room number three as her own personal bedchamber. And its from there that many of the strange disturbances have been reported.

One of the eeriest took place in September 1975, when a radio interviewer was making a tape about the spook. The owner also took part in the recording which was made on a highly sophisticated machine at the usual broadcasting rate of seven and a half inches per second. All the dials indicated that everything was fine. But on playback the tape proved to be blank.

A second recording was made. . .then a third. . .still nothing.

Then on the fourth occasion the voices were recorded but they turned out to be at Donald Duck speed.

If the interviewer had wanted to do that he would have to have moved his machine to record at three and a half inches per second. A special lock on the recorders makes it impossible to change speed accidentally.

The general conclusion was that Marion noted for a sense of humour, was up to her tricks again.

A few weeks earlier the chef had tried to snap a photograph of her when the proprietor offered a reward of £100 for shots of Marion. He broke an ankle after feeling an icy finger push him downstairs.

Another employee quit on seeing a vacuum cleaner fly through the air and an Australian guest asleep in Room Three packed up fast after waking up in the hall. Beer taps have also turned themselves off.

The Phantom Hand

A wealthy laird, cursed by his wife, was murdered at the now ruined Littledean Tower, near St. Boswells, by a phantom hand. . .

A hand which hours earlier he had severed from a witch while she was in the form of a hare!

The astonishing saga began one evening when the laird drove his wife Margaret to despair. She was a kind hearted soul but his frequent beatings and nasty taunts were becoming too much. The crunch came when he declared before a party of drinking friends that a devil from hell would make a better wife and lover.

Margaret stared her husband straight in the eye and with a voice that sent shivers down the spines of everyone present, said: "You will live to regret those words."

Later that night the laird went for a ride on his horse to try and sober up in the fresh air but was forced to find shelter when a storm broke. As the thunder grew louder and the rain heavier he felt himself being drawn to a cottage by some queer force which was hard to describe. The sole occupant turned out to be a stunningly attractive young woman and the master of Littledean was spellbound by her.

After a few more meetings they became firm friends. . .and lovers. They would meet each morning at a small wood near Littledean. When Margaret heard about the affair she decided to confront her rival. She enlisted the help of some friends. In those days Border folk had no time whatever for 'the other woman' who split up a marriage. When caught she would be hoisted on to a pole and put through the degrading humiliation of being dragged through every street in the town or village and then ducked in the nearest water. The angry wives surrounded the circle of trees and then began moving inwards.

No bush was left unturned but the stranger was never found. The only life reported were some birds in the trees and a hare which had been seen scurrying for cover.

Later that night the laird - who could only find friends among the thieves and tramps of Roxburghshire because of his surly manner - was returning to Littledean from a session at local taverns when a party of hares began chasing his horse.

The poor animal was petrified as they jumped into the air and danced before its eyes. Faster and faster the horse travelled but still they were there.

Our laird lunged his sword in all directions as he sped through the moonlit forest but only succeeded in striking one of the hares. Its severed paw fell into his pocket. Then at Midlem - meeting place of witches from miles around - the pursuers gave up their chase.

Once home he spilled the beans to Margaret about the chilling encounter and went to get the paw as evidence. But it now turned out to be a human hand which seemed to be alive. Quickly the laird thrust several stab wounds into the palm and then threw the hand into the Tweed. However it turned up again in the early hours of the morning. This time he tied the hand to a heavy stone and threw it in the deepest stretch of water for miles around. But en route back to Littledean he met another grim sight.

He saw the back of his lover through the trees and shouted to her. She turned round to show a face which was a mass of lines. The lovely girl he knew had aged by 70 years.

Then she held up her right arm. . .it was covered in blood and the hand was missing.

He was a very frightened man but on returning to Littledean there was yet another problem for the hand was back again. This time the fingers that wouldn't die were thrust on to the fire and roasted in the flames. Was this the end?I think not. In the morning servants found our laird lying dead in front of the fire. His throat was covered with marks. Those who saw the body concluded that it had been strangled by a hand.

New Jerusalem

Edinburgh has had many descriptions applied to it in its long and turbulent history, but surely the strangest is the claim that Scotland's capital and the biblical Jerusalem are one and the same place!

The claim is made in "Britain, the Key to World History," written some thirty years ago by Comyns Beaumont, a journalist. Israel's Jerusalem, he says, in no way corresponds to descriptions of the city which appear in the Bible or in the works of Josephus, the Jewish historian of Roman times.

According to Beaumont the geography of Edinburgh tallies exactly with the old accounts of the Holy City. Edinburgh Castle fits the biblical description of Zion, the Citadel, and the Castle moat evidently solves a problem which has puzzled scholars for years. According to II Samuel, "David dwelt in the fort, and called it the City of David. And David built round about from Millo onwards." Experts have never conclusively worked out what or where Millo was in Jerusalem. But Beaumont is confident that it's the moat, which protected the Castle from attack from the Esplanade.

The Esplanade itself corresponds to Mount Opel and the Upper City of Jerusalem, while at the head of the High Street, the Lawnmarket marks the site of Upper Market Place. The ravine now partly filled in and spanned by George IV Bridge is the Tyropoean Valley of biblical times, which was dominated by the great Tower of Antonia, built by Herod to guard the Temple. Hadrian ordered the tower to be razed, and Beaumont claims that the great heaps of debris which formed the foundations for Edinburgh's Mound - linking Princes Street to the High Street - were the long-forgotten remains of the Antonia.

Next come Bezetha and the Pool of Bethesda. Bezetha was a 'new town', built across the Valley of Jehoshaphat and the Pool of Bethesda from the Holy City to accommodate the overflow from Jerusalem's expanding population. Beaumont points to the foot of the Calton Hill and the site of Princes Street as Bezetha. Between them and the Old

Town lie the valley now occupied by Waverley Station and Princes Street Gardens - all that remains of the Nor'Loch, drained when Edinburgh's New Town was built.

Not all of Beaumont's 'proofs' are in the city centre. He suggests that Arthur's Seat - the extinct volcano that looms to the south-east of Princes Street - is in the exact position where the Mount of Olives should be. And Holyrood House, which sits at its base, corresponds to King Solomon's cedar palace, the House of the Forest of Lebanon.

The author sees Joppa as easy justification for his theory. Jerusalem's port has that name, and Edinburgh, too, has its Joppa by the sea, now largely swallowed by Portobello. Beaumont concludes his case by identifying Corstorphine Hill with the biblical Mount Tophet - the Place of Burning - and the Gogar district with Golgotha. The Place of Skulls where Christ was crucified is not in Israel, he claims, but four miles from the centre of Edinburgh.

Beaumont claims that there was a vast conspiracy to place the scene of old Israel's history thousands of miles from where it actually happened. The only thing that's certain about the affair is that Auld Reekie's citizens would be only too grateful for a conspiracy to replace their dreich winter days with Jerusalem's heatwaves!

Eildon's Zombie Knights

The breathtaking view of the Eildon Hills in the distance was probably a key factor which made Sir Walter Scott select the site at Abbotsford for his large mansion home. But records show that the Eildons are more than things of beauty. The three strangely shaped hills are a place of terror as well.

Many legends have grown up around them down through the centuries. What was the truth behind a strange mark which appeared on the hillside at the spot where a man died mysteriously? Are the insides giant chambers where zombie knights exist. . .neither in this world or the next? Why do violent winds blow around the Eildons when the surrounding countryside is calm and quiet? And who is the strange bearded man dressed in clothes from another country?

One of the most intriguing stories in the saga of these hills has its setting in the 18th century. Hawick horse dealer Dick Canonbie was in Melrose for the horse market but had to leave unexpectedly before trading began and dash back home with his animals.

However he got lost in the pitch darkness and decided it would be wiser to rest at Lucken Hare - one of the three Eildon hills - until dawn. As he was about to put his head down for the night a strange old man appeared out of the blue.

He'd spotted Dick's horses and wondered if they wer
"Certainly," replied the friendly dealer.

The stranger, who had a long white beard and old fashi
bought the lot and paid Dick with gold coins which wer
circulation. In fact they'd been used hundreds of years previo.
were still valuable.

He asked Dick to return at the same time the following month and
they'd do business again. Although Lucken Hare was a lonely spot with
no houses for miles around the dealer came back. . .and sure enough the
old man was there.

Again he bought all the horses. Again gold coins were handed over in
payment.

This unlikely business meeting went on for some months until Dick's
imagination got the better of him.

He asked the old man: "Where do you live? Can I see your home?"

The stranger said he was in a hurry but Dick persisted despite a warning
that he might see many things which would frighten him.

After a tiring uphill walk Dick found himself at the secluded entrance to
a cave. He and the old man went in and walked through passageways lit
by torches. Against the wall were horse boxes and in each box. . .a black
horse with a swordsman in armour lying at its feet. It was anyone's
guess whether they were dead or alive.

They then came to a large chamber. In the centre was an oak table
covered in strange symbols. A sword and hunting horn were also there.

The stranger told Dick: "You have been rash to intrude upon the realm
long forgotten by the world of men. Now a choice is forced upon you.
Either draw the sword or blow the horn.

"Choose well and you reign here as king. Choose badly and you forfeit
your life."

Dick selected the horn and as he blew it the entire place erupted in
terrifying howls. The knights and soldiers sprang to life and he found
himself under attack from a furious mob. Then the stranger's voice
could be heard: "Woe to the coward, that ever was born; Who did not
draw the sword before he blew the horn."

Dick was then thrust on to the back of a horse and taken back through
the passages to be thrown out on to the hill. Shepherds tending their
flock found him a few hours later but there was nothing they could do.
However he did manage to tell them about the amazing confrontation
before dying.

Later, at that very spot, a mark appeared on the hillside showing the
outline of a horse and rider.

here have been many reports of a lonely bearded man wandering in the hills. Knights riding ghostly black horses have also been spotted. And howling winds blow around Lucken Hare on the most calm of evenings.

Perhaps all this is appropriate for the three hills which make up the Eildons had a weird 'birth.' The story goes that some 800 years ago a spirit split what was one big hill into three on the instructions of a Borders magician, Michael Scott, who was known as "The Wizard."

Hounded to the Grave

The ruined Buckholm Tower at Galashiels is haunted by the ghost of a fellow called Pringle who owned it in the 18th century.

He was driven to the grave by a phantom pack of hounds after a woman put a curse on him for murdering her husband, Geordie Elliot, and son Willie. Father and boy were Covenantors and consequently, because of their religious beliefs, lawbreakers.

Pringle used to get kicks by sending his dogs into the hills to hunt Covenantors but he went too far when the Elliots were imprisoned in a cell at Buckholm by Captain Bruce of the Dragoons pending trial for suspected covenanting activities.

In the night, blind drunk after consuming vast quantities of brandy, he murdered them both and then strung the bodies through giant hooks which hung from the ceiling.

This beastly master of Buckholm even subjected Mrs. Isobel Elliot to the ordeal of seeing her husband and son's bloodstained corpses.

Needless to say the poor woman didn't know where she was but when Isobel recovered from the initial shock she told Pringle: "May the memory of yer evil deeds haunt ye for ever, like the hounds of hell. May they pursue ye waking and sleeping and may ye find no rest in this life or through eternity."

Her wish came true. The laird of Buckholm never had a night's sleep again. One minute he would be fine the next in complete terror screaming that wild hounds were trying to rip him apart. The noise of hounds could also be heard by folk when they visited the Tower despite the fact that there wasn't an animal in sight.

A few months later Pringle died from the strain after suffering a complete mental and physical breakdown.

But the noises of the hounds, according to some, can still be heard on the anniversary of his death while others say that an exorcism finally put a stop to their awful screeching.

The Devil's Son

A beggar who put a terror curse on the Campbell family from Glenluce, Wigtownshire, was later executed in Dumfries.

Andrew Agnew began his shock campaign after being refused some food when he called at the home of weaver Gilbert Campbell in 1654.

Twice the house was set on fire.

A spirit who described himself as Satan's son appeared and jumped up and down on the floor making the whole house shake. He called out: "Come up father! Come up father!"

Predictions were made about coming events involving the family and as time passed the spirit's statements were proved to be true.

From time to time the house was put under attack by dozens of stones which fired in from all directions through the windows and down the chimney.

Attempts by ministers to exorcise the demon failed and the campaign continued for over two years. Then it vanished for ever. . .just as abruptly as it had arrived.

Boiled in Lead!

The ruins of Hermitage Castle, standing near the Hawick-Langholm road at Newcastletown, Roxburghshire, saw many deaths through murder, disease and suicide during the turbulent centuries when it was occupied by a succession of wealthy Border families.

Not surprisingly the spirits of some of these folk still roam around there today. . .including a former owner who was boiled in lead by angry locals and a sheriff starved to death in the grim dungeons.

William de Soulis, nicknamed the Bad Lord Soulis, was the chap who met his end in a cauldron of lead.

He was an evil man who practised black magic and witchcraft. All sorts of weird and wonderful things happened when he was owner back in the late 13th and early 14th centuries.

Good honest living Borderers hated him and the last straw came when he murdered all his dinner guests one night. One diner did escape but the evil host's men trapped him in nearby water and forced him to stay until he drowned.

King Robert the Bruce was petitioned about the affair. He'd been receiving a barrage of complaints and is apparently said to have told the mob to hang Soulis, boil him or do whatever they wanted.

The vague reply was all they wanted and a day or two later Soulis was thrown head first into the bubbling lead. . .

They rolled him up in a sheet of lead
A sheet of lead for a funeral pall.
They plunged him in the cauldron red,
And melted him, lead and bones and all.

Another story suggests that this is all fiction and that Soulis was in fact arrested for conspiring against the king and sentenced to life imprisonment at Dumbarton Castle.

In the following century Sir Alexander Ramsay of Dalhousie, Sheriff of Teviotdale, was seized by Sir William Douglas and thrown into a dungeon. There he met a slow lingering death. . .by starvation. The ordeal was slightly prolonged by grains of corn which fell into the cell from a granary situated above.

These grains kept him alive for 17 days and it's reported that when part of the old granary wall was demolished in the early 1800s some human bones and a rusty sword fell out.

Another phantom is that of Robin Redcap. The dreaded Soulis had provided him with the key to a buried treasure which as yet is still undiscovered.

Skeleton on Trial

A few miles north-west of St. Abb's are the ruins of Fast Castle where plotters met to kidnap King James VI in 1582. A group of protestant nobles led by the Earl of Gowrie and aided by English funds captured the king and took over governing of the country.

However a year later James escaped and at St. Andrews was proclaimed king. Gowrie was executed but the dramatic culmination of this saga came some nine years later when the skeleton of another Fast Castle plotter, that of John Logan of Restalrig, was put on trial for treason. The bones had been dug from the grave and in court were condemned for betraying their king!

In the sixteenth century Fast Castle had belonged to the Homes family. It came into Logan's ownership through marriage.

Heartbreak!

One of the saddest stories associated with Neidpath Castle at Peebles involves the daughter of an Earl of March who owned it and her deep love for the son of the Laird of Tushielaw.

They wanted to become husband and wife but her parents disapproved. The young man decided the only alternative was to make a clean break and build a new life in a foreign country.

Needless to say the girl missed him terribly and her pain was so great that she fell ill. Eventually the Earl decided that a re-conciliation was the only thing that could save his daughter.

Soon word was received that he would be returning to Scotland and the girl was moved to a house beside the Tushielaw road so that she could greet him as he arrived. There she waited on the balcony but her lover rode past without recognising her. The illness had turned the girl into a pale thin almost pathetic looking figure.

The effect of this killed her and she died in her nurse's arms.

Sir Walter Scott was prompted to write of the affair using these words:-

> He came - he passed - a heedless gaze,
> As o'er some stranger glancing,
> Her welcome spoke, in faltering phrase,
> Lost in his courser's prancing -
> The castle arch, whose hollow tone,
> Returns each whisper spoken,
> Could scarcely catch the feeble moan,
> Which told her heart was broken.

Hello Again!

One of Chirnside's best known characters from yesteryear is Margaret Halcrow, a lady originally from the Orkneys, who married the local minister, Henry Erskine, in 1674.

Her new husband gave her a beautiful ring to mark their union in holy matrimony. It was her most prized possession but tragically just a few months later the young wife of the manse died suddenly.

A last request was that she be buried in the churchyard with the ring still on her finger.

However the village sexton, who'd been left to close the grave after the funeral, opened up Margaret's coffin and tried to steal the ring. But it wouldn't come off.

He then produced a knife to sever the finger from her hand when the corpse suddenly sprang back to life, gave a loud scream and leapt out of the coffin.

She fled back to the manse and banged on the door shouting to her husband: "Open the door, for I'm fair clemmed wi' the cauld."

And from that night she continued to live a long and happy life giving the baffled but delighted minister two fine sons.

A Fatal Error

The partially ruined Spedlins Tower near Applegrath is haunted by a man who died of starvation in its dungeons because of a mistake.

Sir Alexander Jardine, the then owner, was responsible for the tragic blunder.

He had arrested a miller by the name of Porteous for alleged fire-raising and had the man locked up while arrangements were made for a trial.

But the next day Jardine had to travel up to Edinburgh on urgent business and forgot to leave the key. The poor miller had died of hunger by the time the owner got back to Spedlins.

The haunting began a few days later and a minister was called in to exorcise the spirit. The bible he used was placed on a table near the dungeon and the noise of Porteous, pleading for food and drink, stopped. Later, however, it all started up again when the bible was sent away for rebinding.

Strange Pubs!
Greyfriars Bobby

The Greyfriars Bobby at Candlemaker Row, Edinburgh, owes its name to a little Skye terrier who was surely the best pet a man ever had.

Our story begins in the 1850s when a regular open-air market used to be held in the bustling Scottish capital.

Among the hundreds of folk who went there to do business was a shepherd called Jock Gray - he was always accompanied by his dog Bobby.

At one o'clock the kindly shepherd had lunch at Traill's coffee-house while Bobby sat at his feet and tucked into a juicy bone.

Sadly this little tradition, which had gone on for many years, ended suddenly when the shepherd collapsed and died. He was buried at Greyfriars Kirkyard.

A few days after the funeral the proprietor of Traills got a surprise when Bobby turned up at lunchtime. . .begging for a bone. The same thing happened all that week and on the fourth day the coffee-house owner decided to follow Bobby to see where he went after finishing the bone.

Minutes later the man found himself at Jock's grave where Bobby was keeping a vigil - a vigil that lasted for 14 years until the dog's own death in 1872.

Today that coffee-house is Greyfriars Bobby Inn and a statue of the dog stands opposite it.

Burke and Hare

The Burke and Hare at High Riggs, Edinburgh, is named after two rogues who between Christmas 1827 and October 1828, strangled at least 16 people so that they could sell the bodies to an anatomist for medical research.

In the 19th century doctors found it virtually impossible to get specimens, because of the public's attitude to human dissection, and willingly paid out large sums to anyone who could keep them supplied.

Most corpses found their way to the anatomist's table after being taken from the grave by 'bodysnatchers' but Burke and Hare, two Irish labourers who had originally come to Edinburgh to work on the construction of a canal, found their 'specimens' by murdering innocent men and women. They deliberately chose people who weren't likely to be missed - old tramps, orphans, prostitutes and beggars.

Their evil practises were uncovered after a woman's body was found at the home of a prominent city surgeon. In the sensational trial that followed Hare lost his nerve. . .and turned King's evidence. Later he had to flee to Ireland to escape from the furious crowds who wanted to lynch him. Meanwhile Burke was sentenced to death and hanged before a crowd of 20,000 on January 28, 1829.

Perth's Daughter of Satan

Perth woman Isobel Haldane was strangled and burned after a bizarre six day trial in 1623 at which she was found guilty of practising witchcraft.

One of the questions asked was: "Have you ever had conversations with the fairy folk?" In reply she spoke of being taken from her bed some 10 years earlier by a force unknown to her. This forced Isobel towards a hillside which opened up so that she could go inside. There the accused had remained for three days - from midnight on Thursday until the same time on Sunday when a grey bearded man led her out of the 'tomb.'

John Roch was the first prosecution witness. He had been in the local carpenter's shop to make arrangements for a cradle needed for the baby his wife was expecting. Isobel had said not to be in too much of a hurry because the baby would not live. Her prediction came true. Under cross examination she claimed that advance information of this tragedy had been given to her by the grey bearded man.

Evidence was also given that the accused had forewarned a perfectly healthy woman by the name of Margaret Buchanan that she was about to die. A few days later the woman passed away.

Another witness, Patrick Ruthven, told of being bewitched by one Margaret Hornscleugh. Isobel Haldane had removed the spell in a simple short ceremony.

Stephen Ray of Muirton told of turning violently ill after discovering that she had stolen beer from Balhoussie Hall. When he challenged her about this she had declared: "Go thy way! Thou shalt not win thyself a bannock of bread for a year and a day."

The trial also heard of a magic brew made from leaves which cured sick children; of ceremonies involving water from a well and babies' clothing being used to effect cures. In one case some water had been spilled in the street. Isobel regretted this because if anyone stepped over it the child whom she had just cured would again fall violently ill.

Quizzed about the source of her powers Isobel told of being taken from bed, while in labour with her first child, and put in a pond near the door of a house in Dunning. All around fairies were dancing.

Thus, although she had performed a lot of good, Isobel Haldane was considered to be a witch and was sent from the court to her death.

Burning of Dundee Hag

After the Reformation there were demands from all over the country that the practice of witchcraft should be stamped out. To be strictly factual cases of devil worship and strange happenings came mainly out of people's imaginations but Parliament responded by passing an Act in 1563 which made death the penalty for witchcraft. As a result countless innocent women were burned at the stake in towns and villages throughout the kingdom.

Most of the prosecutions in Scotland took place between the Restoration of Charles II in 1660 and his death in 1685.

Dundee Presbytery spared no effort in seeking out the daughters of the Devil. This is made clear by a passage in the Kirk Session records of Auchterhouse as quoted in the "Annals of an Angus Parish" by the Rev. W. Mason Inglis.

It states: "April 27, 1669 - by the orders of the Presbytery of Dundee, action was ordered to be taken against all guilty of witchcraft. The Magistrates of Dundee were particularly desired to use all diligence for trying them further. They complied with the Presbytery's instructions, and appointed those suspected of witchcraft to be banished, which was done, and the Act put in execution."

An old grey haired woman by the name of Grissell Jaffray was burned at the Seagate in November, 1669, as a witch after her powers to foretell future events had been brought to the attention of three local ministers. She was the wife of a local brewer, by the name of James Butchart and had a son who was at sea.

It is said that he had sailed into the harbour on the day of the burning and asked about the smoke which was rising over the town. When informed that it was the flesh of his mother being burned at the stake the young man turned his ship round and made for the open sea. He never again returned to his native parish.

Nine Witches Executed at Forfar

Between 1650 and 1662 no less than nine women were executed in the "Playfield" at Forfar for practising witchcraft. In those days the persecution of witches was carried out with appalling ferocity. Thousands of perfectly innocent folk in towns and villages throughout the country were cruelly put to death on the flimsiest of evidence.

The methods used to extract confessions from suspects were barbaric. Burning with hot irons, pressing of thumbs and legs in vices, and forcing victims to wear iron boots which were alternately heated and cooled were among the least of the harrowing ordeals inflicted by the pious inquisitors of the Church.

People could be strangled and burned on the word of someone who had a grudge against them. Witch-pricklers were employed by the churches and councillors to weed out suspects. Under a licence from the Court of Justiciary they were empowered to go around sticking pins in women suspected of being in league with the devil.

One such fellow was called John Kincaid and the folk of Forfar were so impressed by his efforts that they granted him the freedom of the burgh in 1661.

His method of investigation was simple and is explained thus in "Strange Tales of the Lothians" (Kincaid was a native of Tranent):-

"He would keep sticking the three-inch pin into various parts of the body until the poor soul was in such pain that she could no longer react to a jab. When this happened the spot being pricked was held by Mr. Kincaid to be the "Devil Mark" which, as everyone knew, was immune to feeling pain. Discovery of the mark proved that the woman was a witch. A Lord Advocate of the time described this sign of auld Nick as a small stain which was either red, brown or blue."

Kincaid won fame throughout Scotland as a detector of witches and earned himself a lot of money in the process. But as the century drew to a close common sense began to prevail over all the nonsense that was associated with witchcraft examinations. The pricklers were exposed as cheats and as the pendulum swung Kincaid, once hailed as a hero, was now dismissed as a rogue.

A notable reason for the decline in witchcraft cases was a decision to make individual parishes pay for their own trials and executions. This put an enormous strain on the purses of individuals and thus dampened their enthusiasm for hounding unsuspecting folk to the grave.

By the middle of the seventeenth century it was estimated that Scotland's bill for executions totalled around £100,000 Scots. With the cost of dealing with one witch being as high as £25 it was quite common to dispose of two together and thus reduce the overall bill.

The Devil, who won converts to the art, held parties for them at Candlemas, Beltane and Hallowe'en. He paid them wages in the form of gold coins which within 24 hours turned into horse muck.

During evidence in the Forfar trials it was claimed that one suspect by the name of Helen Guthrie had murdered her half sister who was aged about six or seven. She also confessed to dancing with the Devil and others in Forfar Churchyard. Evidence was also given about a visit by the Devil to Mary Reid's house. He sat at the head of the table in the presence of a large company. Later the party went to the home of brewer Jon Beinny and bought ale.

She also confessed, 'That at the first of these meetings, Andrew Watsone, Marion Rinde, Elspet Alexander, Isobel Schyrie, and herselfe, went up to the kirk wall and raised a young bairne unbaptised, and took several pieces thereoff, at the feet, the hands, part of the head, and a part of the buttocks, and that they made a pye thereof, that they might eate of it, that by this means they might never, as they thought, make a confession of their witchcraft.'

But of course they did. . .and as a result paid a high price.

The Nairn Confessions

The confessions of witch Isobel Gowdie and her companions caused a sensation in the Nairn district. They named many prominent local people of the day as participants in coven rituals which had sex orgies as one of their main features.

Isobel lived in the village of Auldearn and said that she had been baptised into the black art by the Devil himself at a ceremony in the parish church. Along with her coven leader John Young she admitted casting spells over farmers' fields so that their sect would get the benefits of the crops whilst growers got nothing.

Under cross-examination by officials she explained why those women who indulged in supernatural practices were not missed by husbands when they went out in the middle of the night to attend coven meetings. The witches simply placed a broom or stool in the bed, whispered a short spell and the object took on their appearance. To reach the rendezvous point they put a straw between their feet, recited a short rhyme and flew off.

Isobel confessed to being involved in an attempt to murder the parish minister, Mr Harry Forbes, whilst he was ill. The flesh, entrails and gall of a toad, a hare's liver, grains of barley, nail parings, and bits of his clothing were all steeped in water and put in a bag. While this was being done the Devil stood chanting: "He is lying in his bed and he is sick and sore. Let him lie in that bed two months and days three more. He shall lie in his bed, he shall be sick and sore. He shall lie in his bed two months and days three more." The coven members also joined in the chant whilst on their knees and as they spoke they raised their hands towards the Devil. Bessie Hay, one of the witches, was sent into the minister's room with the bag. But good Christian folk were there visiting Mr Forbes so the spell was effectively broken.

Other admissions which were made in the year 1662 included attempts to harm the children of a local landowner, the Laird of Parks, with images. No conclusive record exists to prove whether Isobel met the usual witch death of burning at the stake but judging by her claims, whether true or imaginary, she certainly made every effort to achieve just that!

The Aberdeen Witches

Aberdeen suffered an attack of "witch fever" in the late 1590s. The year 1594 saw several women being sent to their deaths at the stake. In 1596-97, no fewer than 24 women and two men died as a result of executions or tortures. These unfortunate people had been held prisoners in the kirk. Two women died before being brought to trial. Cause: Starvation and continual prodding with sharp stakes.

Locals were pleased. An entry in the Council Register of September 21, 1597, states: "The quhilk day, the prowest, baillies and counsell, considering that William Dun, dean of gild, has deligentlie and cairfillie dischargit him of hes office of deanrie of gild, and hes painfullie travellit (laboured) theirin to the advancing of the commoun gude, and besyddes this, hes extraordinarlie takin panis on the birning of the gryt number of witches brint this yeir, and in the four pirrattis, and bigging of the port on the brig of Dee, reparing of the Greyfreris kirk and stepill thairof, and thairby hes ben abstractit fra hes tred of merchandice continewallie. . .theirfoir in recompence of hes extraordinarie panis and in satisfactioun theirof (not to induce any preparative to deanes of gild to crave a recompance heirefter) but to incurage utheris to travell als diligentlie in the discharge of their office, grantit and assignit to him the soume of fourtie-seven pundis thrie s. four d. awand be him of the rest of his compt. of the unlawis (fines) of the persons convict for slaying of blakfische (kelts) and dischargit him theirof be thir presentis for ever."

Charges brought against witches in old Aberdeen were wide-ranging. They included dancing with the devil round the market cross, using supernatural powers to make husbands unfaithful to their wives, and developing a potion which rendered other victims impotent.

Janet Wishart, an elderly soul who died in the flames, was accused of casting spells on an Alexander Thomson and an Andrew Webster. Both men had complained of suffering from severe fits of shivering followed by fits of sweating. Webster eventually died from the effects. Besides this the indictment against Wishart made reference to numerous other unspecified deaths as well as acts of witchcraft which included using burning coals to raise storms and of creating monster cats to frighten chosen victims.

A woman named Isobel Crocker was burned along with Wishart. Old records detail the costs of execution:-

Item:

For 20 loads of peat to burn them	40 shillings.
For a boll (six bushels) of coal	24 shillings.
For 4 tar barrels	26 shillings 8 pence.
For fir and iron barrels	16 shillings 8 pence.
For a stake and dressing of it	16 shillings.
For four fathoms of tows (hangman's rope)	4 shillings.
For carrying the peat, coals and barrels to the hill	8 shillings 4 pence.
To one justice for their execution	13 shillings 4 pence.

Witches at North Berwick

A plot hatched in East Lothian to end the life of King James VI by witchcraft resulted in many men and women being burned at the stake. Amongst them were John Fian 'alias John Cunningham, maister of the Schoole at Saltpans'; Agnes Sampson of Haddington who flew into North Berwick on a sieve; and Euphemia Macalzean, a very wealthy and influential lady of the day.

In 1591 enquiries uncovered the activities of three covens at North Berwick. Under the leadership of Fian they had been busy planning the king's death. The first group were under orders to obtain a bit of his clothing which would be wrapped round a wax image then burnt. Another group were to try and poison him and the rest were invited to raise storms in an attempt to sink a ship carrying James and his new Queen from Denmark.

The first two schemes came to nothing it seems and the Royal party completed their sea crossing quite safely although sudden storms were encountered en route. However, a ship loaded with jewels which had been bought by His Majesty for the Queen sank not far from Leith after being caught in a freak gale. At a subsequent trial the witches were found to have been the cause of changes in the weather. It was said they had flown out over the Forth on sieves. A cat, which had parts of a dead man tied to it, was christened 'king' and dropped into the water to create the storm. At this point it should be mentioned that the many charges brought against Euphemia Macalzean included "drowning a boat betwixt Leith and Kinghorne, wherein were 60 persons lost." The king was said to have escaped death at the hands of the witches because of the pious life which he led.

But his treatment of Macalzean was decidedly un-Christian. She was burned alive on July 25, 1591. He did not allow the usual 'courtesy' extended to witches of strangulation before being put on the fire, because of her Catholic religion.

John Fian faced 20 charges at his trial with the plot against the King forming the basis of the main ones. It was said that he held his coven meetings in the parish church at North Berwick. Access was gained by Fian's use of a 'Hand of Glory' i.e. the hand of a murderer cut from the corpse on the gibbet, dipped in wax and used as a candle. This gave him the power to open all kinds of locks. Other charges against him included stealing bodies from the churchyard and cutting them up for use in ceremonies.

To extract confessions those in authority put the schoolmaster through horrific tortures. Rope bound round his head was tightened until he screamed with pain. The torture of the boots was used until his "legs were completely crushed and the marrow spouted out." Pins were stuck into his body and the Devil's mark was found under his tongue. Death came eventually on the stake at Castlehill, Edinburgh, and one can't help feeling that it must have been something of a relief for him.

Agnes Sampson told investigators of going to sea on sieves with 200 other witches and landing at North Berwick on Hallowe'en. She gave details of meetings with the Devil in the churchyard and of grave robbing. And James was amazed when Agnes was able to give a verbatim account of the conversation which had taken place in private between him and his wife on their wedding night. The other 53 charges against her included having advance knowledge of deaths, curing disease through the use of charms and of course raising the storm to kill the King. She was executed on Castlehill.

Much of the information which nailed the North Berwick witches came from a lass by the name of Geillis Duncan who was a maid-servant to Tranent magistrate David Seaton. She had extraordinary powers of healing and was described at the time as a good hearted soul always ready to help those "greeved with any kinde of sickness or infirmitie."

But Mr Seaton, who in law was responsible for the activities of his staff, became alarmed by rumours that Geillis was dabbling in witchcraft. She was tortured by him and forced to confess involvement with a coven. One of the instruments used on her was the "witches' bridle." This consisted of an iron hoop which was placed over the head and tightly padlocked in position. From it extended a piece of metal with four points. Two were forced to press on the tongue and palate and two pressed out on the cheeks.

This and other sinister objects led the servant girl to start naming names and so keep the fires outside Edinburgh Castle burning for many a day.

Devil Worshippers

Six Bo'ness people were burned at the stake in 1679 after a bizarre trial at which they had stood accused of practising witchcraft and being in league with the Devil. The evidence included submissions that he had: played the bagpipes at a dance they held at the Murestane Cross high above Killeil; made them cast spells to kill the baby son of an elder at Kinneil Parish Church; and drank seven gallons of ale in a house at Grangepans after roaming the town disguised as a dog.

The five women and one man were arrested on Hallowe'en. The evidence given would be laughed out of court nowadays but our misguided forefathers in Borrowstounness, as the town was then called, did not hesitate when it came to returning a guilty verdict. Later nearly the entire community turned out to see the 'victims' - an appropriate word under the circumstances - being dragged from their cells in the

Tolbooth to face the sentence of the court. One can only imagine how they must have felt at seeing the stakes on the shores of the Forth, the hungry flames from the fires and the accusing jeering taunts of their dreadfully misguided contemporaries.

Against this background it is not surprising that another Bo'ness witchcraft trial, held a few years later, ended abruptly when the accused woman, Anna Wood, made a dramatic escape from custody. Her troubles started after local sailor Robert Nimmo made a series of complaints to the Kirk Session of Carriden Church.

He said that Anna was a witch who had threatened to kill him one dark winter evening as he was walking home over the hills from Linlithgow. She first appeared with five other witches in the form of black cats. They spat and hissed at him in a menacing manner. Later the witches turned themselves into human form and then birds.

By next morning the eerie encounter was the talk of Bo'ness. In his evidence to the elders of the kirk Nimmo also said that Anna Wood had haunted his ship. This prompted other seamen to come forward and make similar allegations. Anna even turned up aboard ships while they were anchored in distant overseas ports. And each appearance always preceded an accident or the disappearance of goods. On one occasion a cabin boy fell overboard and was drowned.

Euphaim Allan, who employed Anna as a serving maid, didn't help. She confirmed that the girl had been out of the house at the time of the alleged appearances before sailor Nimmo. The trial was then adjourned for the day but next morning it had to be abandoned completely after the clerk announced that the accused had escaped. Clearly this was the only option she had of carrying on living as it is not difficult to imagine what the outcome of the trial or the sentence of the court would have been.

Devil Worshippers

Burn her Alive

A bite from a dog helped convict Helen Rogie of witchcraft. And the sentence of the court was: 'Burn her alive!'

She was known as the 'Witch of Findrack' and belonged to a coven which met regularly near Torphins. Rogie was arrested after cursing wealthy farmer John Mackie and his family. Their dog died suddenly, a few hours after biting her. A few days later Mrs Mackie fell and broke a leg. Then the daughter of the house died.

These, along with other mishaps and tragedies which befell neighbours, made the basis of Rogie's summons before the Assizes on charges of practising witchcraft. She received advance warning, presumably through supernatural sources, that a party of arresting officers were on their way to her cottage, and fled. The unfortunate lady managed to evade capture for some days before being traced to a cave in the hills. Earlier, a search of the cottage had found pictures of the people she had cursed, images cut in soft lead, strange writings, twisted wire and coloured threads.

At the Assizes, presided over by John Irvine of Pitmurchie in April, 1597, it was decided that Rogie be taken to the Gallows Hill at Craigour to be burnt. Expenses were agreed - 66 pence to cover pay for the hangman and funds to provide twenty loads of peats, a boll of coal, four barrels of tar, four fathoms of rope and a stake.

Naughty Monks Burned Alive

Dead Man's Gold

A fourteenth century blacksmith called Osbarn was one of the North-East's most evil sons. His treachery and lust for money led to an entire garrison of his countrymen being butchered by the English in September, 1306.

Osbarn was a blacksmith serving the little community of Greenstyle, nestling on the southern slopes of Ben Newe, and the mighty castle of Kildrummy. Business was excellent and he made handsome profits attending to the military horses and other needs at the castle.

But Osbarn, a greedy selfish character who didn't have a friend in the world, was always trying to make more and more money. He wanted to be one of the richest men in the kingdom and was determined that nothing and no one would stop him reaching his goal.

In the summer of 1306 certain events occurred which were to drastically affect his life and those of many others. King Robert the Bruce had been defeated at Methven near Perth. He managed to flee and make for Aberdeen. There Robert was met by the Queen, daughter Marjorie and brother Nigel. Other Scots swelled the numbers of the Royal party but it was forced to move west because of the continuing advance of the English.

As the days passed Robert came to the conclusion that the struggle was going to be very bitter and tough so he sent the ladies to Kildrummy Castle for safety under the escort of Nigel and the Earl of Atholl. However bad news awaited the party there when it was learned that Edward of Carnarvon, son of the infamous Edward I of England, was heading north. The Queen and her ladies fled to the sanctuary of St. Duthac's Chapel at Tain. Nigel Bruce stayed behind to lead the defence against the enemy.

Plans were made to deal with the attack and Osbarn was kept busy checking all the ironwork of the castle. Any weak points in this area would give the English an obvious advantage.

On August 1 Edward set up camp at Kildrummy. Then the campaign to storm it began. Attack followed attack but the brave Scots stood firm. The days turned into weeks and still the English couldn't make any headway.

All this time our greedy blacksmith was busy planning and plotting. If the English won the garrison would surely be put to the sword and that would be the end of his business. If they lost things would revert to the status quo and he would be no better off. So, in an attempt to drastically alter the situation, Osbarn sneaked out of the castle late one night and headed for the English camp. He explained his business to a soldier and was taken to meet the Prince. The English then devised a plan on how to seize Kildrummy with his assistance. But the smith was a bit put out when it emerged that part of the scheme would involve him setting it on fire. He hadn't planned on having to do anything which might be so risky. Osbarn demanded a suitable reward and let out a howl of delight when Edward told him: "You will have as much gold as you can carry." All he had to do was return to the castle and await the signal to start the fire.

This came a few days later and Osbarn threw a piece of red hot metal on to the thatched roof of the great hall which was situated near to his forge. The flames spread very quickly and the garrison was thrown into a state of total confusion. The brave Scots, once they had recovered from the initial shock, managed to seal up the openings caused by the fire. Unfortunately their food and ammunition had been destroyed in the blaze. So tragically it was hunger and not the English which forced them to surrender in early September.

Nigel Bruce was hanged at Berwick and the rest of the garrison were all butchered. Proud as a peacock Osbarn went to claim his reward. But a big shock was in store. The English tied him up, forced open his mouth and poured molten gold down his throat. They had kept their word. The greedy smith got as much gold as he could carry. . .

Doomed man's cry...

Public hangings used to attract large crowds. In Dundee spectators came from all over and jammed the streets of the town hoping for a glimpse of the unfortunate 'victim' drawing his last breath.

An important feature of these occasions was the doomed man's farewell speech. This usually took the form of a final declaration of innocence.

Street porter Arthur Wood, who had been convicted of murdering his son John, left the 10,000 crowd in no doubt as the death rope hung over his neck at five minutes past eight on the morning of Monday, March 25, 1839.

In a loud and clear voice he declared: "I go before a just God to answer for my sins; but the crime I am here to suffer for I know nothing of it. I was not, to my knowledge, in the sight of God, either art or part in that crime.

"I never entertained a thought of it at any time, and I die freely without any knowledge of that kind before God.

"Neither did my companion, to my knowledge, entertain any such thought, or was art or part in the crime. It was said that she was the cause of quarrelling in my family; this I never knew anything of, now that before God I stand."

The companion he referred to was his second wife Henrietta. They had three children and lived in Monk's Court, Thorter Row. John was his son by a previous marriage.

Despite Arthur's death speech neighbours knew that Henrietta and John did not get on at all well and they constantly had rows. In the early hours of Sunday August 5, 1838, Duncan McNab, nightwatchman, was passing through Monk's Court when he heard what appeared to be a fight in the Wood's house. Such disturbances were not uncommon at this spot as three public houses had back doors leading into the Court. He called out 'past one o'clock' and went on his way.

A neighbour, Mrs. Scott, heard the rumpus and at one point Arthur Wood declared: 'I'll be your butcher before I sleep.' Then there was silence.

As the steeple clock struck 1.30 a.m. she looked out of her window and was shocked to see the Woods' carrying out John. He appeared to be lifeless. They laid him on his back at the foot of the stair. Mrs. Scott concluded that the young man was probably drunk and had been put out in the open to sober up.

Around 15 minutes later McNab came into the Court and with the assistance of a passerby called William Annal, he examined John. They found that the lad was dead.

Subsequent police investigations established that he had been strangled.

A search of the family home revealed several pieces of rope and when applied to the dead man's neck one of them fitted the red groove which was made during the murder act.

Arthur Wood, a one-time successful auctioneer who gave way to drink after a bad business deal, and Henrietta were arrested. Their trial had to be delayed because she was pregnant but after the baby was born in Dundee Prison it opened at the High Court, Edinburgh, on Monday, February 25, 1839.

Arthur was a popular man in Dundee and the trial was watched with great interest. In evidence the couple contradicted each other. Wood said that his son had not been at the house that night. Mrs. Wood, on the other hand, declared that he had been there but she refused to let him in.

There were no witnesses for the defence. Mr. Neaves, for the Woods, made a plea for a verdict of 'not proven.' But the jury, by a majority of 14 to one, found Arthur guilty. By nine votes to six they found the charge against Henrietta 'not proven.'

The judge ordered his execution for March 18. Dundee was in uproar and a petition was organised. This delayed the execution but the Home Office then said that nothing could be done.

So Arthur Wood went to meet his maker. . .and left the folk of Dundee with a speech to debate and think about for a long, long time afterwards.

Lie to the corpse - if you dare!

When tramp Thomas Scobbie was arrested after the murder of an Angus gamekeeper he was subjected to a bizarre test which used to be a feature of Scots law. The 35-year-old Fifer was put face to face with the corpse and asked: "Did you ever see that man before? Did you murder him?"

Usually the strain of such an ordeal made killers crack but Scobbie maintained his cool and replied: "No! No! I'm bad and bad enough, as the polis ken, but I'm no' a murderer."

The whole sorry affair began on the morning of September 24, 1872, after some washing was stolen from the garden of a house at Kingennie. It was occupied by gamekeeper George Spalding, 42, and his family. When informed about the incident by his sister the gamie set out to look for the culprit. The most likely candidate was a tramp who had been seen acting suspiciously near the house earlier on.

George eventually caught up with the tramp who, after a stormy scene, was forced to produce the clothes from a hiding place. But he denied stealing them and tried to put the blame on a friend. The gamekeeper was not happy with the explanation and decided to take him to Monifieth Police Office. En route Scobbie tried to escape but was caught by George's dog Juno and pinned to the ground.

Later a violent argument developed between the two men. The gamekeeper became extremely abusive, it was claimed, and Scobbie, in a rage, strangled him. As he fell to the ground George hit a stone which badly damaged his head.

All this happened around 4 p.m. in the afternoon. When he didn't return home that night the Spaldings were not unduly concerned. His job often took him away from the house at all hours of the day and night. But by 8.30 next morning they began to get worried. Juno had come home alone and it was long past the time for George's breakfast.

They called in Dundee Police and the descriptions given of the tramp pointed to Thomas Scobbie. He was so repulsive in appearance that folk gave him the ironic nickname of Bonnie Scobbie.

The tramp was arrested. An examination of his clothes showed that a pair of trousers had been torn by what appeared to be the teeth of a dog. A shirt had blood marks on it. Friends whom Scobbie had visited in the Overgate on the night of the murder confirmed that his face had been badly scratched and covered in blood when he called at their home.

Despite his denial of murder when brought face to face with the corpse Scobbie was charged and by 14 votes to one a jury at Dundee Circuit Court found him guilty at a trial held in the following April.

They recommended mercy but the judge Lord Deas issued the following sentence: "In respect of the said verdict of Assize against the panel, Lord Deas and Lord Jerviswood decern and adjudge the said Thomas Scobbie, panel, to be carried from the bar back to the prison of Dundee, therein to be detained, and fed on bread and water only, until Tuesday, the 29th day of April next to come, and upon that day, betwixt the hours of eight and ten o'clock forenoon, within the walls of the said prison, to be hanged by the neck upon a gibbet by the hands of the common executioner, until he be dead, and ordain the said body thereafter to be buried within the walls of the said prison, which is pronounced for doom."

There was a lot of sympathy amongst members of the public for Scobbie whom it was generally felt had been provoked beyond reason. More than 4300 signed a petition which was forwarded to the Home Secretary.

On April 25 a reprieve was granted and the sentence was changed. ."To be detained during Her Majesty's Pleasure."

The main reason, however, for this was not sympathy for Scobbie but to cover up a blunder by Lord Deas. For when writing the sentence the judge forgot that April had began (it was the 8th). The phrase "next to come" was most unfortunate because there would not be a "Tuesday, 29th of April next to come" for six years after that. To wait so long would have been quite wrong so it was generally agreed that the best course of action was to pay heed to the petition.

Scobbie was released from prison in 1897 and returned to his home town of Dunfermline where he died a short time later.

Murder Most Foul!

William Burry told friends that he and his wife Ellen were off to start a fresh life in Australia. But the ship they took from London - along with some luggage and an empty packing case measuring three feet by two feet six inches by three feet - was bound for Dundee and not Down Under.

The 29-year-old sand merchant planned to bring his wife to this "remote place", murder her, and then return home to claim the remainder of a £300 inheritance left by Ellen's aunt.

What he didn't know was that the money had already run out. This was mainly due to his refusal to work since publication of the will and his excessive drinking habits. And he was also wrong if the thought crossed his insane mind that the citizens of Dundee were a bit on the simple side.

Burry lured his unsuspecting wife to Scotland after showing her a letter which he had invented. Dated January 12, 1889, it was supposed to have come from the firm of Messrs. Malcolm, Ogilvy and Co. It stated: "We, Messrs. Malcolm, Ogilvy and Co. Ltd., Dundee, do hereby agree to take into our employ w.h. and e.n. Bury, of No. 3 Spanby Road, London, E. for a period of 7 years. Wages for W.H.B. £2 per week; wages for E.B. £1 per week. To enter on duty as soon as possible. Travelling expenses wil be allowed after one Month from Date of entering employment."

More intelligent women would have spotted that the letter was a fake but Ellen was taken in. Once in Dundee they rented a two roomed house at 113 Princes Street. They remained here from January 29 until February 4 and didn't mix with the neighbours.

At lunchtime on Monday, February 4, Burry went to a shop at 125 Princes Street and bought a piece of cord. He was said to be "quite sober" at the time. That night he attacked Ellen and knocked her partly unconscious. The cord was tightened round her neck and pulled until the last ounce of breath had gone. Not content with this Burry plunged a knife into the lifeless woman. Bloodstained clothes were burned on the fire and the body was put in the packing case brought from London. This was to be her coffin. To get it in the limbs were twisted to a shocking degree. The box was nailed down but Burry's problem now was to get it out of the house. Day after day he   racked his feeble brain trying to think of a solution.

Eventually he cracked and went to the Central Police Office in Bell Street. Burry told the duty officer that he and his wife had ended up hopelessly drunk the previous Monday. Next morning he found her lying dead on the floor. For some reason, which he couldn't explain, a knife came into his hands and he plunged it into her body several times.

The sergeant found the story obviously astounding and could only conclude that the man was either drunk or mad. Lieutenant Lamb was despatched to the house where the body was found.

Burry was charged with murder and at the subsequent trial in Dundee Circuit Court the jury rejected his plea of Not Guilty. On April 24, 1889, he was executed at Dundee Prison.

The Braemar Sacrifice

Hundreds of years ago in Braemar, the Castle of Kindrochit was a popular residence for Scottish Kings who came to the north on hunting expeditions. Constables who governed it had considerable feudal powers over the local population and the incumbent of the post during Malcolm Canmore's time chose to exercise his authority in a somewhat peculiar fashion. Families were ordered to provide him with a live cow on a rota basis which he used to feed a wild boar.

The beast, kept as the castle 'pet', was called Tad-Losgann and was a great source of amusement to Malcolm during his frequent visits. . .particularly as it had always grown quite considerably!

Farmers in the area, who at the best of times had a terrible struggle to make ends meet, bitterly resented this plunder of their stock but were powerless to act. Then one day something happened which so to speak was the straw to break the camel's back. Sandy McLeod, a lad of some 15 summers and much respected bowman throughout the district, was very angry when the Constable chose his widowed mother's cow to feed Tad-Losgann. In hard financial terms it represented more than two years solid work and she was heartbroken by the decision. Neighbours could only offer sympathy but Sandy decided on a positive course of action. He would kill the beast!

Later that night and outwith his mother's knowledge he made a set of special arrows. After dawn part one of his plan was implemented when the first arrow was used to shoot a large capercailzie. This was to be the bait which would draw Tad-Losgann from his den.

Sandy hid the capercailzie near his home until nightfall. Then after darkness he set out. The young archer skilfully avoided being seen by the castle guard and once within shooting distance of the den he hurled his carcase towards the boar. Hours seemed to pass and nothing happened. Then Tad-Losgann appeared and followed the scent. Within a few seconds Sandy had the perfect shot and without hesitating he fired. The arrow went straight through the beast's heart. Death was instantaneous. Sandy managed to get back to his mother's cottage in Glen Slugan without being spotted. Once inside he collapsed into a deep sleep totally exhausted.

Next morning the news spread like wildfire and local folk, delighted at the end of the cow sacrifices, hailed the mystery killer as a hero. The Constable was, of course, not amused. He ordered a search of every home in the district. The arrow taken from Tad-Losgann's heart was matched up with arrows found in the McLeod cottage. Sandy was taken prisoner and confessed to the 'crime'. He was sentenced to die on the gallows on Creag Choinnich the following morning.

Coincidentally the king was due to arrive for a visit at around the same time. The Widow McLeod was heartbroken and blamed herself for all that had happened. She decided that a reprieve from the king was their only hope and set out to meet the Royal party. Malcolm, when he heard what the widow had to say, promised to make enquiries on his arrival at Kindrochit. After hearing the facts he decided that Sandy should have a chance of life. His mother was to be put on a rocky ledge across from the castle with a peat balanced on her head. If he could pierce it from the castle drawbridge freedom would be the prize. The lad was trembling with fear but knew this was his only hope.

The Widow McLeod smiled at her son and gave him as much encouragement as she could. Sandy took aim. . .fired. . .and knocked the peat off her head. The watching crowd gave squeals of delight and King Malcolm congratulated the lad on a "splendid" shot. He also promised Sandy a place in the Royal Archers when a man. But this was not to be for young McLeod never fired another arrow in the rest of his long lifetime.

Buried Gold

At Carmyllie there is said to be a stone which turns three times when the cock crows. The legend of the Cauld Stane o' Crofts is that it fell from the Devil's belt whilst he was in the district. There is also a suggestion that the stone fell from a witch's apron.

Another local folktale concerns a crock of gold and a buried castle. The gold can be seen from a certain point when the sun is shining but the route to it has not yet been discovered.

Morphie, near Montrose, was haunted by a urisk - half man, half goat - whilst the North and South Esks boasted water kelpies which captured unsuspecting travellers and then promptly drowned them.

A cave named as the Dragon's Den near Perth is known in legend as the place where Brude, the sixth century Scottish king, slew such a creature in order to win favour with St. Serf.

Hundreds of folk used to gather there on the first of May each year to celebrate a Pagan festival. It was eventually declared undesirable by the church and made illegal.

Hanged for cutting a tree

Legend has it that a man was hanged - for cutting a piece off a Spanish chestnut tree at Careston Castle near Brechin. The tree was famous and the laird was so furious at the actions of Jock Barefut that he had him strung up from the same tree.

But after the death penalty was carried out it withered away. Later the spirit of the dead man began to appear on the road between Careston and Finavon. Jock's ghost was full of mischief and played many tricks on unsuspecting passers-by.

Perthshire has several legends connected with the apparition of the bean-nighe, or washing-woman. To see the washing of the death-shroud at the side of a river or loch was believed to be a forewarning of death.

In the county the washing-woman was described as a creature, small and rotund. Folk who spotted her shouldn't run away. Instead an effort should be made to creep up behind the bean-nighe and ask her for whom the shroud was intended.

North-East Castle Spirits

The ruined Rait Castle near Nairn is believed by some to be haunted by the ghost of a girl who has no hands and wears a blood-stained dress. She is a daughter of the Cummings family who were the owners at one time.

A bright, intelligent girl she was very much in love with a member of the Mackintosh family. Unfortunately they were despised by her father who had hatched a plot to lure his enemies to a banquet and once inside Rait murdered them all. The plan came unstuck and the girl was accused of tipping off her lover.

As a punishment for this alleged 'betrayal' the chief of the Cummings family cut off both his daughter's hands. The poor girl was at her wits end and the sheer horror of what had happened drove her to suicide.

Down through the centuries there have been occasional glimpses of her troubled spirit moving amongst the ruins.

Ghosts with no heads have been reported at Dunphail Castle, south of Forres. One of them is the spirit of an Alastair Cummings, who along with several companions, managed to escape from the fortress while it was being besieged by the Earl of Moray.

Later they succeeded in getting supplies of meal into the castle to feed the starving clansmen within. Sadly, the daring heroes were captured and beheaded. Their heads were thrown over the castle wall by Moray's men who cried: "Here's beef for your bannocks!"

Years later during excavation of a nearby mound, five headless skeletons were found.

During 1571 Corgarff Castle, some 15 miles north-west of Ballater, was the scene of mass murder. While her husband was away, the mistress, Margaret Forbes, plus 26 relatives and servants were burned to death in a retaliatory raid by the Gordons.

Not surprisingly the 16th century tower house, converted into a garrison post and enclosed within a star-shaped wall in 1748, was said to be a haunted place after that.

Ghost of Borthwick

Borthwick Castle, near Gorebridge, built in 1430 is reputed to be haunted by the troubled spirit of a young girl from a previous century. Helen Bailey who now occupies this 15th century fortress and who has always been sceptical of supernatural happenings, witnessed the re-enactment of the macabre torture and killing of the young servant girl, who was left to die in the now haunted room.

Her experience has been reinforced by other guests who have reported strange happenings in this particular room. The temperature would suddenly drop and sometimes frantic scratchings would be heard on the inside of the door. Although the door had been painted, the scratch marks have reappeared at a time when there were no animals living in the Castle. Two gentlemen visitors from Chicago stated that the heavy fire door opened on its own volition during the night and remained open until it was closed by one of them. Footsteps are frequently heard on the spiral staircase leading to the haunted room, usually around 1.30 a.m. During a conference of business men, sobbing and wailing was heard in the same area although all the occupants of the Castle were in the Great Hall at the time.

An artist from Edinburgh who visited the Castle repeated word for word the same description of how a girl dressed in medieval costume had met her death. The basis of his story is exactly similar to that of Miss Bailey's, namely that the victim was a serving girl who was with child. She was held by either witches or midwives whilst a soldier cut her across the abdomen with his sword and abandoned her to an agonising death.

Borthwick Castle has had a turbulent past, as turbulent as Scottish history itself.

In days of old, there was a different source of terror for English soldiers who found themselves unfortunate enough to be taken prisoner and placed in the dungeons at Borthwick. Those who wished to secure their release were invited to jump between the twin towers of the Castle. Success in making the 12 foot leap would be rewarded with freedom. However, there was a considerable handicap - the prisoners had their hands tied behind their backs and were compelled to make a standing jump from one tower to the other. The 110 foot drop did little to inspire confidence. There are no records available of any prisoners having successfully negotiated this impossible challenge.

Borthwick Castle is internationally known for its historic and romantic association with Mary Queen of Scots and the Earl of Bothwell. In 1567, the Queen and Bothwell fled from Edinburgh and sought refuge at the Castle. James Hepburn Earl of Bothwell was suspected of murdering Lord Darnley, the Queen's second husband and that Mary had conspired in his death. The house in which Lord Darnley had been sleeping was blown up and his strangled body found under a tree close by. Suspicion mounted when three months later the Queen married the Earl of Bothwell.

In a history book of Borthwick Castle, Helen Bailey writes that the marriage "fanned the flames of suspicion but it also strengthened the resolve of the Loyalists who were convinced that she had to be rescued from Bothwell's evil influence before irreparable damage was done to her cause and theirs.

The sixth Lord Borthwick, loyal to his faith and his Queen, did not hesitate to place his Castle stronghold at the disposal of Mary and her accused husband.

On the morning of June 11th a force of some thousand men led by Lord Home, surrounded the Castle. Bothwell who was aware that capture would mean instant death, escaped leaving Mary behind.

Then occurred one of those happenings that is the essence of which romantic history is made. While as evidence of their good intentions towards the Queen, Home's forces were withdrawing, Mary, disguised as a page boy, climbed through a window in the Great Hall, lowered herself by rope to the ground below and set off through the postern gate and across the glen in search of her husband.

Had she remained under the protection of the Borthwicks' the subsequent events would have been different but this was the path she chose. Her reunion with Bothwell was a short one. He was defeated by the Lords at Carberry Hill on June 15th and fled the country later to die unloved and unmourned in a Danish prison.

Queen Mary never again knew real freedom. She had been caught in an irreversible chain of events that led inevitably to the ignominy of death by beheading on February 8th, 1587."

Eighty years later a further chapter was added to the tempestuous history of Borthwick. Oliver Cromwell beseiged the Castle and forced Lord Borthwick and his family to surrender to his forces.

It is not surprising that strange and unexplained happenings occur which cause the unbelievers in the supernatural to wonder, as there is no rational or scientific explanation that can be given.

Man with Three Bodies

St. Baldred did much to spread the word of Christianity in the Lothians many centuries ago but when he died at the East Lothian parish of Auldhame a problem arose. They wanted the privilege of enshrining his remains but so did the neighbouring communities of Preston and Tynninghame.

Tradition has it that St. Baldred, anxious to avoid being a cause of controversy, performed a miracle from "the other side" because on the night of his death his body became three. Thus all three churches were able to be his tombs.

During his lifetime St. Baldred was credited with removing a crag, dangerous to the navigation of the Forth, with all the ease of steering a small boat. It later became known as St. Baldred's Rock.

The Angry Spirit

Two men had to stand trial after allegations of murder were made against them by A GHOST! They were accused of murdering an English sergeant by the name of Arthur Davies. The spirit of Davies, who had vanished while on a solo hunting trip appeared almost a year later before shepherd Alexander MacPherson. In a dramatic statement he pleaded for a decent burial and after giving the location of his remains, named his killers as Duncan Clark and Alexander Bain MacDonald.

They were both known to be Jacobite sympathisers and as such had an obvious motive. For Davies was a sergeant in the English Army and with a team of men had been sent to Aberdeen after the fiasco of the Second Jacobite Rebellion to ensure that the local Scots were kept well and truly in their place. This was done through a number of measures such as the banning of the kilt and other forms of tartan dress.

A few hours before being killed Davies, while on patrol in the Braemar district caught John Gowar of Glenchunie wearing a tartan coat. The sergeant gave Gowar a severe rocketing. It was to be his last reprimand. That same day murder struck and Davies, who always dressed well and carried plenty of money, was robbed of every penny and other items of value which were on his person.

But in death he was determined to get justice and returned to Braemar where he appeared before MacPherson. MacPherson wasn't helpful, so the sergeant then appeared before an Isobel MacHardy, who was the wife of the shepherd's employer. That started things moving. There was a proper funeral, then Clark and MacDonald were arrested. However, at their trial in Edinburgh (1754), the evidence against them, although strong, was not enough to warrant a conviction. The case ended with both men being acquitted.

Frightening Encounter

An East Lothian landowner who died with a guilty conscience returned from the grave to seek assistance from the parish minister of Innerwick. While still of this life Maxwell, Laird of Coul, had swindled relatives out of large sums of money by forging certain documents. He now wanted the minister, a Mr Ogilvie, to get in touch with his widow and have arrangements made to pay all the money back. Only then could he rest in peace.

But, despite several approaches, Mr Ogilvie refused to become involved in the affair. In fact throughout the remainder of his lifetime he never spoke a word to anyone about the spirit's pleadings. It was only after his death, when papers were being sorted out at the manse, that the Laird's visitations came to light. A book was subsequently published, based on the papers, and it became an eighteenth century best seller. It was earnestly studied and debated by academics of the day who regarded the contents as an important insight into life in the hereafter.

The story began on the night of February 3, 1722. Mr Ogilvie was riding home when suddenly a figure appeared from the shadows and bellowed: "I am Maxwell, Laird of Coul. And I want you to do a good action on my behalf. However, I see you are in no state to discuss anything. I shall come again when you are more composed."

The ghost's comment was something of an understatement because Ogilvie was nearly dead from fright. He barely managed to make it back to the manse. However as time passed he got over the shock and the pressure of other parish affairs pushed the matter to the back of his mind.

A full month passed before the Laird made his second appearance - on the road to Blarehead. Mr Ogilvie refused to consider any pleas for help until the ghost answered certain queries. This time, completely composed he fired a barrage of questions.

Asked if he was happy the phantom Laird replied: "I have not yet appeared before the Maker to be judged." Next question: Where do the unjudged wait? The Laird replied that good souls were happy with their clear consciences and looked forward to a future of bliss. The wicked suffered from the realisation that their lifestyles on earth had been wrong and they feared severe punishment. Asked if people had guardian angels Coul confirmed: "Indeed they do! And attendant devils as well!" Angels had different abilities, just like ordinary men, and were given jobs which best suited these. The angels would meet regularly to discuss various matters but at such gatherings no lies could ever be spoken.

The Laird then vanished into thin air. Then four weeks later he appeared before Ogilvie at a ruined building near Oldhamstocks. Here the request was made to approach his widow and sort out the money which had been swindled. But the minister said he could be of no help and rode off. On the journey home Ogilvie became conscious that someone was following him. He pulled into the side and when the shadow of a horse and rider appeared he called out: "Who's there?" Back came the reply: "Maxwell, Laird of Coul. Be not afraid." Ogilvie thought it was someone playing a joke but when he raised his cane and brought it down on the figure it sliced straight through to the ground.

The next night Coul again appeared on a path at Pease Bay and asked the minister's help. Ogilvie feared that he could end up being sued for slander if he repeated the statements without proof so he demanded that the instructions be made in writing. This, for obvious reasons, was impossible. The minister refused to assist and Coul, who was very angry, thundered off into the night. And that was the last appearance of the ghost with a conscience.

Phantom Pilots

During the First and Second World Wars reports were made of ghost sightings at the aerodrome in Montrose. The first spectre was said to be that of a lieutenant who was killed outright in May, 1913, after his biplane fell from the sky and crashed at the perimeter of the airfield. It burst into flames on impact leaving practically no trace of remains or wreckage.

Soon afterwards the pilot's ghost began appearing around the airfield. Story is that his plane had been deliberately tampered with during a repair and he was unable to rest in peace because of the double-cross which had led to his death. In August, 1916, a major saw the ghost on no fewer than five occasions and several instructors made reports of sightings during the autumn of that year.

The ghost has also been up in the sky on his phantom plane. One evening base officials sent a Hurricane out to investigate what appeared to be a buzzing of the airfield by an enemy aircraft. The pilot found nothing but later had to abandon several attempts at landing because an ancient biplane kept getting in the way. . .More recently, in 1963, the plane was seen crashing to its end - 50 years to the day of the actual accident.

One morning during the Second World War an officer, based at the aerodrome, was killed after his plane went out of control. He was strict on discipline and rumour had it that a fitter decided to take revenge on the pilot for a public bawling out by fixing the plane in such a way that it would never make another journey.

Nothing was ever proved to this effect but not long after the accident the pilot's ghost began to appear and was spotted by various base staff.

A Slave's Curse

When Andrew Lammie and Agnes Smith met it was love at first sight. Sadly however for them a happy marriage and children were not to be. For Agnes was the daughter of a very wealthy and proud local miller who wanted her to wed someone rich and influential. Andrew was as poor as a church mouse and his job of trumpeter at Fyvie Castle, Aberdeenshire, in the eighteenth century, didn't offer any prospect of sudden prosperity.

The miller banned the young couple's courtship but they continued to meet in secret. All was well until the jealous laird of Fyvie stepped in. He too had fallen for the miller's daughter but she'd spurned his advances. This was more than the laird could take and he decided to hit back after hearing about the meetings by having Andrew transported to the West Indies as a slave!

The young trumpeter lived and worked there in wretched conditions but after a few years he managed to escape and made his way back to Scotland. Never a day had passed without the love of his life being in his thoughts.

Sadly, however, she was not there when he came home. Agnes had died of a broken heart during his absence. The strain of getting back coupled with the long hours of toil as a slave had taken their toll on Andrew. Once strong and firm he was now weak and the tragic news drained from him the will to live.

A short time later he died and on his deathbed cursed the Laird of Fyvie, swearing that a trumpet would sound every time a laird was about to die. The story goes that the haunting of Fyvie began a short time later and for many years afterwards the death of a laird was preceded by a trumpet blast in the stillness of the night.

Another ghost which has been linked with Fyvie in the past is that of a Green Lady but her origins were a mystery.

This fourteenth century castle has an interesting story to tell about the famous Scots wizard Thomas the Rhymer. He cursed all future owners after being refused a night's shelter there by declaring that the place would never descend in direct line for more than two generations.

The man who whipped up the wizard's anger was Sir Henry Preston of Craigmillar, the then owner, and a noted participant in the battle of Otterburn (1388). He was upset on the day of the Rhymer's visit over demolition work which had gone wrong and snapped that no room was available when the request was made for accommodation. As it happened a small crowd, familiar with the great reputation which Thomas had in matters magic, had gathered outside the castle to see him. Now they were given first hand experience of him working a curse!

The sky turned black and the clear sunny day gave way to a terrible thunderstorm. The wind howled around the castle and everyone watching got a real soaking. Yet the spot where Thomas stood remained bone dry and there wasn't a speck of rain on him.

From what is known of owners in the few centuries that followed it would seem that his curse operated effectively.

The Black Colonel

John Farquharson, one of the seventeenth century chiefs of Inverey Castle, was known as "The Black Colonel" because he was a tall dark man and a fearless fighter.

One of the proudest moments of his life came with the Battle of Killiecrankie when he raised a small army to fight alongside Viscount Dundee. Many of his men died but the Black Colonel managed to escape and flee back to Inverey with the Redcoats in hot pursuit. He cleverly sidetracked up Glen Ey and took shelter in a cottage while the enemy tried to storm the castle. Eventually they got inside and were furious to learn that Farquharson had evaded them. As a 'punishment' the building was set on fire and the chief's retainers were all butchered.

The Black Colonel however had the last word. Before going into battle he had filled a room with gunpowder and as the fire spread there was a mighty explosion which blew many of the Redcoats to pieces. Later after gathering more men the Black Colonel took the remainder of the enemy on in a skirmish at Braemar. He won and they were driven from the district.

But Farquharson was not content with simply being a controversial and colourful figure in life. Even after death he still made his presence felt.

The story goes that the Colonel's final wish was to be buried in the family graveyard at Inverey. Well-meaning folk however decided that he should go to his last resting place with chieftain's honours at Castleton of Braemar.

This was done but the day after the funeral puzzled passers-by found the coffin lying beside the grave which only hours earlier had been filled in. Three times the coffin was buried. And three times it mysteriously rose. His followers decided to take it to Inverey. The road was blocked because of a landslide so a raft was made to float it down the Dee. He was laid to rest in the family graveyard and there was never again any trouble from the Black Colonel.

Water of Miracles

A Celtic missionary called St. Monire played a key role in bringing the message of Christianity to Deeside. But he nearly died after being viciously beaten up by the simple natives who lived in the hamlet of Auchendryne where he had gone to spread the word of God. They had been told by their pagan priest that St. Monire was an evil spirit who could cause great trouble if allowed to stay. This terrified the locals who attacked the missionary with sticks and stones.

Saddened and badly bruised St. Monire fled for his life. He travelled along the banks of the Dee and by nightfall had reached Inverey. Unfortunately word from the pagan priest got there before he did with the result that his requests for a little food and shelter against the bitterly cold night were refused.

The missionary was an elderly man who had been advised by friends not to make the hazardous journey into the wilds of Aberdeenshire and now he was beginning to think that they were probably right. St. Monire decided to press on but on the slopes of Carn Na' Moine collapsed from sheer exhaustion. Death seemed inevitable and the next morning he could hardly move at all.

The pagan priest, who was hiding near by, watched cheerfully as the dying Christian groaned in agony. Then a miracle happened. A stream of sparkling clear water began flowing out of the rocky hillside. St. Monire crawled towards it and began drinking. With each mouthful he grew stronger and stronger. A few minutes later St. Monire was as fit as a fiddle!

The pagan priest then appeared and declared: "That stream will be cursed as it has fed the thirst of an evil spirit!" He called on the Pagan Gods to dry it up and threw mud on to the source to stop it flowing. The stream vanished.

St. Monire calmly replied that it had been blessed in the name of the Virgin Mary, said a short prayer and the water began bubbling forth again. The priest was astonished and begged forgiveness. St. Monire had won his first convert. For centuries afterwards folk who were sick and ill came from all over to partake of the water and many cures were claimed because of its magical properties.

After turning Auchendryne into a Christian community St. Monire moved on to Crathie where he built a church. Following his death in 824 an annual fair was started in his honour and held on December 18 each year. St. Monire also worked among the people of Balvenie in Banffshire where a church was built.

A Child Corpse

In the early 1900s a baffling ghost story unfolded in an elegant hotel situated near Aberdeen's St. Swithin's Street. One of the rooms was occupied by a tourist who was dying slowly and painfully from what a doctor described as "a very loathsome Oriental disease fortunately rare in this country." All the hotel staff knew about her was that she had at one time been an actress and had arrived at the hotel while suffering the first effects of the illness. She registered under the name "Miss Vining."

A certain Nurse MacKenzie was called in to look after Miss Vining's needs. The hotel itself had been recently modernised and the new decor impressed the nurse. But when she entered Miss Vining's room there seemed to be a dramatic change in the atmosphere. Nurse MacKenzie suddenly felt very depressed and downhearted yet there was nothing concrete to account for her feelings. The same thing happened when she went on duty at 8 p.m. the following evening. It was a wild and stormy night outside and Nurse MacKenzie decided to pass the time by reading. Two hours later she looked up from her book and was surprised to see a small girl sitting on the chair beside Miss Vining's bed. Assuming that the child had slipped in unnoticed the nurse was about to ask her to leave when the child raised a hand. This seemed to cast a spell over our Florence Nightingale who now takes up the story. . .

"She motions me back. I obey because I cannot help myself. Her action is accompanied by an unpleasantly peculiar expression that holds me spellbound. . .

"Her face turns towards Miss Vining, but she wears a very wide-brimmed hat and I can see nothing of her features. I gather she is both beautiful and aristocratic. Something in her serpent-like ease suggests the East. . ."

Meantime Miss Vining was rolling about the bed going through terrible physical and mental torture. Her temperature had shot up to an alarming 104. Then the child suddenly vanished.

On the third night Nurse MacKenzie was given strict instructions not to allow any visitors so she locked the door behind her and settled down by the fire. Aberdeen was again bitterly cold and the streets outside were covered in snow. The nurse was glad to be indoors and feeling snug and warm she began to doze off. But sobbing from the bed jolted her awake. The child was there again and held up her hand towards Nurse MacKenzie who collapsed "spellbound and paralysed" as her patient moaned in terror. When the child walked towards the window a few minutes later the spell appeared to be broken. The nurse now demanded to know who she was. There was no reply and Nurse MacKenzie snatched the wide-brimmed hat from her head. But it just vanished into thin air. Then the nurse found herself staring into the face of a Hindu child whose throat had been cut.

Nurse MacKenzie fainted from shock. When she came round the child had gone and Miss Vining was dead.

Later the nurse looked through her patient's possessions in the hope of finding some information which might lead her to relatives who would need to be informed of the death.She was intrigued to come across a large envelope marked "Quetta". Inside was a picture of a Hindu child and Miss MacKenzie recognised the dress immediately. It was the one worn by her phantom visitor! On the back of it were the words: "Natalie, may God forgive us both."

Advertisements were placed in newspapers seeking further information but there was no response.

The Hindu child was happy with her revenge, it would seem, because no child ghosts were ever seen in the hotel after Miss Vining's death. But there were reports of a woman ghost in the building.

Charming the Rain

Throughout the North-East various ceremonies were observed to try and influence the weather by making it either rain or shine. A typical example of this from Banffshire was recorded by James Mackinlay in "Folklore of Scottish Lochs and Springs" published in 1893.

It states: "At Botriphnie, in Banffshire, six miles from Keith, the wooden image of St. Fumac used to be solemnly washed in his well on the third of May. We may conclude that the ceremony was intended as a rain-charm. It must have been successful, on at least one occasion, for the River Isla became flooded through the abundance of rain. Indeed, the flooding was so great that the saint's image was swept away by the rushing water. The image was finally stranded in Banff, where it was burned as a relic of superstition by order of the parish minister about the beginning of the present century."

Miracles of St. Giles

St. Giles Cathedral takes its name from a renowned medieval saint who performed many miracles. He is understood to have been born at Athens in 640 and to have died some time between 720 and 725, on the first Sunday in September. For centuries this date was regarded as one of the most important on Edinburgh's calendar and an annual procession was held through the streets in his honour.

Egidius, to give St. Giles his Latin name, is thought to have performed his first miracle by placing his coat over a sick man whom he met on the way to church. This had the effect of producing an immediate and total recovery.

Later a special prayer saved the life of a fellow who had been subjected to a deadly serpent bite. On another occasion a service was interrupted by the screams of a man whose body had been possessed by an evil spirit. Egidius drove it out by using his extraordinary gifts.

All this brought fame but he preferred anonymity and was constantly on the move around Europe in search of peace. A cave in the Gothic forest near Nimes provided the perfect sanctuary. Here he lived on roots, herbs and the milk of a hind.

One day the hind was chased by hounds belonging to the King of France and driven into the cave. There Giles was discovered. Later, when he told his story, the king decided to erect a monastery there and gave him the title of abbot. He held the title until his death.

One of the most interesting works to be compiled on the cathedral and the saint's life story was written by William Chambers in 1879.

Mr Chambers says: "Numerous churches and other ecclesiastical establishments, also hospitals, were founded in his honour. In England alone there were 146 churches dedicated to St. Giles.

"His fame having reached Edinburgh, he was adopted as the patron saint of the church."

During the reign of James II an arm bone, said to be that of St. Giles, was brought to Scotland and gifted to the church. This was enshrined in silver and kept among the treasures of the church until the Reformation.

Phantom Ploughman

A ploughman who refused to help a trapped man found himself a total outcast for being so selfish. No one in the Penicuik area, where he lived, would have anything to do with him. His girlfriend broke off their relationship and his employer gave him the sack. In total despair the ploughman, whom we will call Andrew, took his own life. Death, however, did not bring peace for his troubled spirit returned to haunt the Mount Lothian Quarry, five miles south of Penicuik.

It was near here in the nineteenth century that Andrew had refused to be a Good Samaritan when he came across a toppled cart. The driver, who was pinned underneath, groaned in agony and begged him to get assistance. But Andrew refused. He had borrowed his master's horse without permission to make a surprise visit to his girlfriend's home at Eddleston and was terrified of being found out as such an action was punishable with instant dismissal. Late that night the ploughman again passed the accident spot and by this time the carter was very weak and freezing with the cold. Still Andrew could only think of himself and refused to help.

Seven hours later the driver was found by a group of lime-burners who were on their way to work at the quarry. But their initial shock at the carter's condition turned to anger when they heard about Andrew's refusals to help. They began talking of revenge but he begged them to do nothing. As it happened this was to be his final wish because a few moments later he died in one of the men's arms just as the cart was being lifted off his crushed legs.

As news of Andrew's despicable action spread he became hated and despised. The carter had been well liked locally and no one could understand how the young ploughman could have been so heartless. The strain of it all became too much for Andrew and he killed himself. Not surprisingly few tears were shed when he was buried in spare ground where the estates of Roseberry and Whitehill met.

Soon afterwards his ghost began to appear at the quarry and down through the years numerous sightings were reported by workmen.

Ghost of Death

In days gone by there was a tradition of a death bogle which jumped out at unsuspecting passers-by on a road near Pitlochry. Travellers who were touched died within a year. Accounts of its appearance do not tell us whether the ghost was man, woman or beast. Once a victim had been selected it would move in at fantastic speed.

At one time a house stood by the point in the road where the ghost made most of its appearances. This house was said to be haunted. An evil spirit would control a candle which gave chase to an occupant. Such an occurrence was also a forewarning of death.

The Magic Pear

Adam de Gifford was a wizard living at Yester around 700 years ago. He had a daughter who courted a Broun of Coalstoun. They made plans to marry after a while and the young man asked the wizard what sort of wedding gift he planned to give.

The father of the bride replied by producing a pear. He handed it over to the groom saying: "This is my daughter's dower. As long as it is preserved your lands, which will go to her descendants, will remain intact."

The instructions were followed religiously and, with the pear, passed down from generation to generation. But centuries later a female member of the Broun family tried to bite a piece out of the fruit. Her teethmarks made quite an impression and soon after some of the land had to be sold. . .

Rogues Retreat

The West Lothian village of Torphichen used to be a haunt of highway robbers, tricksters and killers. For a one-mile radius around the monastery of the Knights of St. John of Jerusalem was an official sanctuary. Once inside the circle, marked out with boundary stones, fugitives were free from the usual processes of law.

The knights had possessions in most countries but their chief seat was at Torphichen. They marked the centre of their sanctuary with a stone which had a Maltese cross carved on top. Many chases across country ended abruptly at the boundary stones although of course once inside the fugitives did have to put their case to the knights.

The Order arrived in Linlithgowshire in 1124 and built their priory with the consent of King David I of Scotland. A writer in the New Statistical Account mentioned St. John's Well, at a distance to the east of the monastery where the knights used to go "in days of yore for a morning draught." The waters were said to possess curing properties and could also be used as a charm.

Ghost of the Cliffs!

Wealthy heiress Isobel Fraser was heartbroken when her father banned all contact with the man she loved. It was yet another example of the bullying which made life unpleasant for all who lived and worked some centuries ago at Wine Tower - a solid building of several storeys overlooking the North Sea near Fraserburgh. As far as the laird, Sir Alexander Fraser, was concerned he was right about everything and anyone who opposed him on a point just had to be wrong.

Isobel found life lonely and miserable until a stranger called John Crawford knocked on the door one evening. Outside a snowstorm was in full blast and the visitor explained to the doorman that he had been en route to visit relatives when his horse went lame.

Isobel's father was away on business for a few days and she gave instructions to servants that Mr Crawford was to be given food and shelter. Later they met for a chat and Isobel was surprised to find herself face to face with a handsome young man of around her own age. They got on very well and talked long into the night. This was just the first of many meetings and their friendship grew into love. But all dates had to be conducted in secret because Sir Alexander disapproved of the young man.

One day, however, he received information about a rendezvous and locked Isobel in her room. His men were then sent off to arrest John who was put in chains in a cave below the tower.

That night the sea was very stormy and water which swept into the bleak 'dungeon' drowned the prisoner. Next morning, unaware of the tragedy, Sir Alexander, took Isobel down to the cave. He wanted to teach them both a lesson by showing who was boss. Inside they found the cold and lifeless body.

It would be an understatement to describe the scene which followed as an angry one. Isobel accused her father of many things, including murder. She then went up to the top of the tower and jumped off. . drowning in the sea below. Sir Alexander never recovered from the double tragedy which his actions had produced and became a virtual recluse for the rest of his life.

The story has one final twist. It is said that these events are not unconnected with the appearance, from time to time, of a phantom who roams the clifftops stopping every so often to listen to the sounds of the birds and of the sea. . .

Camp Meg

Camp Meg

A woman who lived in the "Roman Camp" above Mayfield, Dalkeith, in the nineteenth century was thought by many locals to be a witch because of her ability to be in two places at the one time. They named her "Camp Meg" and it's said that a fortune she accumulated is still buried in the woods to this day. Her stay in Midlothian makes fascinating reading and here we produce an account of her life and times which was first published in "Village Story". . .

Meg made a lot of money using her extraordinary powers as a "cattle doctor." She held three surgeries a week - Penicuik on Tuesday, Dalkeith on Thursday and Haddington on Friday. She rode from her lonely cottage deep in the Camp on Skewball - prizewinner at many contests including Dalkeith Fair. Most folk were convinced that Meg bewitched her horse. During races she would spur him on by repeating the same phrases over and over: "Talla, Tall, Ada, Daum, Daa." Meg claimed that the Devil visited her regularly at the Camp. She described him once to some frightened villagers: "His face is as old as the hills and is red and blue in colour."

Collier John Rigby, in an essay written on Meg in 1850, tells us: "It was said by some that she was seen gathering sticks in the Camp Wood, and when they looked in at her window, they saw her, at the same time, busy spinning at her wheel." Meg had arrived at the Camp 35 years earlier.

Her real name was Margaret Hawthorn and she had come to Midlothian from Galloway. Meg started off life in a happy home and had loving parents. In her early twenties she met and fell in love with a wealthy landowner. After a whirlwind romance they married and set up home on a large estate. Their happiness was complete when Meg gave birth to a son. But a few years later the husband died suddenly. He left Meg the entire estate although a neighbouring landowner falsely claimed part of the property as his. He conducted a vicious campaign to try and force the young widow out. Eventually her patience snapped one morning when she saw the imposter striding over her land. She drew a pistol and shot him. Meg immediately realised the possible consequences of her crime and so made arrangements with some close friends to look after her son. She then fled from the district to begin a very new life - as a fugitive from justice.

For many weeks Meg travelled over hills and through valleys looking for a safe place to hide. Eventually she arrived at the Roman Camp, found a tumbledown cottage called Wartstone and moved in.

To reduce the risk of detection Meg wore men's clothes - a large hat, vest, coat, long trousers, and a pair of old wellington boots. Her only real companions were Skewball the horse and a bulldog called 'Help.'

Children were so terrified of 'the witch' that organisers of the bi-annual Caledonian Hunt gave her the job of keeping unruly youngsters out of the Hunt path. They admired Meg's rugged character and always organised a special collection for her before the start.

Although a frightening figure of a woman Meg was respected and well liked in a special kind of way by a lot of folk in the Esk Valley so her death during a severe snowstorm in 1827 saddened many a heart. Her funeral took place at the graveyard at Newbattle but it wasn't the way she wanted to go. Not long before dying Meg had sold her body to a Mr. Laidlaw for medical research and received a fee of twenty shillings. The arrangement was that he would bury her remains beneath a large hawthorn tree near her house with the following inscription on the tombstone:

Caledonia's huntsmen now safely may scamp,
Since their heroine's gone, the pride of their camp,
Her bones are at rest now, her soul's on the tramp,
In the valley of Death thro' yon deep dreary swamp,
May she be guided safely thither by a Lamp - the Lamp of Glory.

Ghost Piper of Arbroath

Smugglers are blamed for spreading a story about a phantom piper who could be heard marching below ground at Arbroath. Tam Tyrie had taken shelter in a cave about three miles from the town with his wife and dog. Later the droning of his pipes was heard at a farmhouse and other places well inland from the sea. It was spooky hearing the old Highland tunes coming up from below the ground.

General explanation for the story is that smugglers, who used local caves for hiding their goods, spread it about to keep intruders away.

At Invergowrie there is an unusual legend concerning the Devil. This place apparently was the venue for the first Christian church on the north side of the Tay. Auld Nick, in a bid to stop it being completed, fired giant stones over the water. Two fell short while a third zoomed more than half a mile past the church to become known as the Devil's Stone.

Thomas the Rhymer, in a prophecy about these stones, says:

"When the Yowes o' Gowrie come to land,
"The Day o' Judgement's near at hand."

The Devil was also involved in frequent controversy with Jean, the Witch-wife of Cardean, and a well-kent fae in the Meigle district. Her cottage home was on the banks of the Dean Water near to the Witches Knowe. She effected many cures and was particularly good at sorting cattle ailments. Although a witch, and presumably a servant of the Devil as such, she wasn't afraid to disagree with her master and they had frequent quarrels.

Ten Heads and Ten Hands

Ten Covenantors who were executed after fighting in a bloody battle at the foothills of the Pentlands provided the authorities with an additional spine-chilling warning for anyone thinking of rallying to the cause. For after the hangman's rope had been removed from their lifeless necks the heads of the ten were cut off and despatched for display in various parts of the kingdom. The right hand of each victim was also chopped off and these were sent to Lanark and fixed to the Tollbooth.

This was just one of the grim after effects of the Battle of Rullion Green in November, 1666. The ill-equipped Covenantors, who were fighting for a Presbyterian system of church government, free of state interference, were hopelessly outnumbered by the regular troops led by Dalyell of the Binns. The weather was very bad and the severe frost and snow nearly froze many of them to death before the fighting had started. Most had little more than an old musket in their hands and a meal-poke on their backs. One account put their total ammunition at sixty muskets, forty pairs of pistols and twenty pounds of loose powder. Claims have also been made that even after the battle had ended in the anticipated overwhelming defeat of the Covenantors Dalyell's men then set about cruelly murdering many of the wounded. Others were robbed of what little they had and bodies were stripped of clothing. Next morning the womenfolk of Edinburgh came out with fine household linen and buried the dead in shrouds. Later a monument was erected over their grave.

Accounts as to the number of Covenantors who died in the battle vary. One historian put the figure at 50 with 80 others taken prisoner. Other books speak of scores of men being butchered and as many as 120 prisoners.

After the battle many managed to escape and all that night the Pentlands must have been a place littered with anxious and frightened fugitives. Many dramatic stories built up around the escapes of individuals and for generations afterwards provided a fund of bedtime stories for mothers to tell their bairns.

Captain John Paton was the hero of one such yarn. He was galloping over the hills towards freedom when three soldiers appeared and gave chase. Soon they had caught up with Paton and one grabbed his coat. But just ahead lay a wide treacherous pool out of which three other Covenantors were already pulling their horses. With a mighty leap the captain's horse leapt over. He then swung the nag round and flashed his sword into the air. In one stroke the head of the first cavalier was split open. The other two came tumbling off their horses and the murky waters became the grave of Paton's enemies and their horses. As his attackers prepared to meet death Captain John galloped off into the night calling out: "Take my compliments to your master and tell him I cannot sup with him tonight!"

Ten Heads and Ten Hands

The Burry Man and Evil Spirits

Strangers who happen to be in South Queensferry on the eve of the annual Fair are likely to get a shock - by coming face to face with an unearthly looking creature who has a thick rough "skin" which is anything but human. But this is no demon from the deep or invader from Outer Space. It's merely the Burryman on his rounds.

His unnatural appearance comes from a head-to-foot coat made up of sticky burrs collected from the Scots Burdock plant. The Burryman makes his walkabout each August as part of South Queensferry's Fair celebrations. His face, arms and legs are covered in flannel and the complex process of putting the burrs on takes hours. Two companions are needed to prop up his arms, which must be extended sideways, as he walks around the town. Burgh householders are then visited and requested to make a donation. It is considered to be unlucky to refuse.

The origins of this ancient custom are not known but one theory is that the Burryman was created by our ancestors to patrol the parish boundaries and ward off evil spirits. Some experts point to the Little Leaf Men who are part of ancient festivals in certain Continental towns. When winter departs and the trees become green again a youth is selected by his contemporaries to be entwined in branches taken from the trees. He has two companions and they visit all the local houses asking for gifts and food which go towards a huge feast for youngsters of the area. In times past Jack-in-the-Green men were common in English parish festivals. The chap chosen as Jack went around with a wooden frame over his body which was covered in greenery.

Bury Me Alive!

Edmund Graeme was shattered when told that his bride-to-be had been unfaithful to him. And not long afterwards he died of a broken heart.

On hearing of the tragedy the girl was full of remorse. She gave instructions to servants that the body was to be taken in a double coffin to a grove in the Vale of Strathmore, Forfar, which had been their favourite rendezvous. It was also there that Edmund had first learned of her affair.

The servants arrived at the pre-arranged time of midnight. They had been puzzled by the girl's peculiar instructions but the reason for her request started to become clear when she emerged from behind a tree wearing a white death shroud. The girl climbed into the coffin beside her dead fiance and ordered the bearers to nail down the lid. They obeyed and thus the young couple were laid to rest together.

Later the girl's spirit began appearing in the area. She always materialised before young ladies who were out walking on their own. And the same message was always given: "Never be unfaithful to your man. . ."

Spectre at Penicuik

Spectre at Penicuik

The phantom of a broken-hearted girl whose life ended suddenly in the early 19th century has been seen in certain parts of Penicuik. For the purposes of our story we will call her Morag Mackintosh.

Morag was the daughter of a local farmer. He had chosen a young man to marry her but she barely liked her father's choice far less loved him. To add to the difficulties of the situation Morag was introduced one day to a young French officer who was a prisoner of the Napoleonic War. Along with his fellow countrymen the officer was held at a mansion house called Greenlaw - today Glencorse Barracks occupy its site.

The prisoners were allowed a fair bit of freedom and could go out for walks alone provided that they did not stray more than a mile or two. It was on one such occasion that Morag and the Frenchman met. They got chattering and as the weeks passed became firm friends. Then their friendship grew to love. Mr Mackintosh hit the roof when he heard about the relationship and banned them from seeing each other.

Morag pretended to accept the ultimatum but continued to meet her lover in secret. One evening they were walking hand in hand through local woodland when Mr Mackintosh and the man he had chosen as a future son-in-law came striding down the pathway towards them. Father and spurned suitor were furious at seeing the couple together. They attacked the officer and viciously beat him to death. Morag, sobbing frantically, was carried home and locked up in the hope that she might be more composed by morning.

But later that night she fled from the house and was never seen alive again. Next day a search was launched when her disappearance came to light. It ended with the discovery of Morag's body at the foot of a rocky gorge on the North Esk. This spot soon became known throughout the entire district as Lover's Leap. Down through the years there were numerous reports of her troubled spirit being spotted at the murder scene and in the area where her life ended so suddenly.

Miracle in the Sky

Flag in the Sky

There is a fascinating legend that the flag of Scotland - a white St. Andrew's cross on a blue background - had its origins at the East Lothian village of Athelstaneford where soldiers about to go into battle saw a vision in the sky. Hungus, king of the Picts, and Achaius, King of the Scots, prayed for victory in their forthcoming struggle against the Saxon king Athelstan. As they were asking for God's help and support a huge white cross appeared in the blue sky above them.

This proved to be a good omen because Athelstan lost the battle and from that day on the Scots carried the flag of a white cross on blue.

A version of the legend from 200 years later tells that Hungus and seven of his men were nearly blinded by a 'divine light.' Then the voice of St. Andrew was heard from heaven. He said that the cross of Christ would move before them as they marched against the enemy and bring success in battle. When the confrontation took place next day St. Andrew's prophecy came true.

Mystery at an Execution

Did some supernatural force intervene as David Balfour was about to be hanged and send people in the 18,000 crowd sprawling and screaming in all directions?

Many of the folk who were assembled in Dundee for his execution in June, 1826, were in no doubt that something very odd indeed had happened.

This was the first execution in the town for over 20 years. Balfour, 39, convicted of killing his wife, was led up to the Guild Hall and bound there. He was then marched through the westmost window on to the scaffold.

A hymn was sung and he gave a short speech. As the hangman was about to do his duty there was a sudden movement towards the west end of the High Street. One account written after the incident says it was "as if a bombshell or some object of terror had fallen amongst the crowd. Men, women and children were overturned, screaming and sprawling in all directions. No sooner had quietness been restored than a similar panic occurred immediately under the scaffold; and the uproar was renewed.

"Amid all the turmoil Balfour remained unmoved. And at ten to three the bolt fell. His tragic story was ended.

"For many years afterwards the mysterious panic at Balfour's execution was regarded by the superstitious as a supernatural interposition."

Blow the House Down!

Blow the House Down

To Scots folk of the 1970s Tam Dalyell is the popular and hard working Member of Parliament for West Lothian. Some 300 years ago his ancestor of the same name was also a well-kent figure up and down the country - but for very different reasons. Legend has it that the seventeenth century Tam enjoyed playing cards with the Devil even though the games often ended in bitter controversy. Venue for these meetings was the beautiful country house of The Binns at Philipstoun.

On one occasion the Devil took the huff after losing and threw the table at Tam. He ducked in time and the table flew straight out of the house and ended up at the bottom of sergeant's Pond in the grounds. In the late 1870s the pond water-level plummeted because of a drought and a heavy card table, which was stuck fast in the mud, became visible for the first time. The discovery generated new interest in the tale which had been passed down from generation to generation.

The table can now be seen at the Binns. In the 1930s, Eleanor Dalyell feared that the heavy marble top might fall on a child, since the legs were rickety. So she asked James Turnbull, joiner from Bo'ness, to put sturdy kitchen table legs on it. At the time he said: "This is a very interesting bit of work for me. It's one of my last jobs as I am nearly 70. One of my first jobs was helping, as a laddie, to pull your table out of the pond!"

A row over cards has also been given as the explanation for the turrets which stand at each corner of the Binns and serve no useful purpose. They were built by Tam to pin the walls down after the Devil, annoyed at losing yet another game, threatened to blow the whole place apart. Tam Dalyell is said to have replied: "I will pin down my house and my walls with a turret at every corner." In fact, this is the Kremlin type architecture of North Russia that Tam Dalyell would have seen in exile at Twer, Novgorod or Tallin.

It's also claimed that his ghost has been seen in the area and a tiny little phantom wearing a brown cloak is said to gather sticks on the hillside above the Binns.

Tam was head of the armed forces in Scotland and in 1681 he formed the regiment which became famous throughout the world as the Royal Scots Greys. . .now the Royal Scots Dragoon Guards. Today the Binns is in the ownership of the National Trust for Scotland and Tam M.P. still has his home there.

Miracle on the Traprain Law

Miracle on Traprain Law

A miracle on Traprain Law, East Lothian, helped lay the foundations of Scotland's biggest and most powerful city - Glasgow. For at the beginning of the sixth century the entire district was governed by a pagan king called Loth. He was an extremely bad tempered fellow and his people were terrified to step out of line. Loth's family were ruled strictly but the harsh treatment turned his daughter into something of a rebel. She was named Thenew and incurred his extreme displeasure by becoming involved with a young Christian. To make matters worse she ended up expecting his child and Loth was furious.

He decided that she must die for her 'sin' and ordered a group of followers to take the girl to the top of Traprain Law and throw her over the steep side. The fall should have crushed Thenew to pieces but she got up and walked away without so much as a single scratch. Next Loth had her set adrift at sea in a tiny fragile boat. The vessel should have remained afloat for only a short time yet it safely carried the spurned daughter over the stormy waters to Culross in Fife.

On the shore there Thenew gave birth to her child, a son, and was later found by the monks of St. Serf. St. Serf adopted the child as his own and named him Kentigern. The name means Chief Lord but later he was given a pet-name Mungo which means the 'Lovable Man.' And it was of course this St. Mungo who went on to write the first chapter of Glasgow's history by establishing a religious institution on the banks of the Molendinar around 550.

Buried Treasure

Buried treasure! That was the cry that went out from Traprain Law in more recent times. For in 1919 an archaelogical dig took a sensational turn when a mystery silver object was discovered. It was a little bowl and further investigations uncovered a pit. Inside it were a hoard of dirty coloured objects and the entire area reeked of sulphurous fumes.

Later, after intensive studies, it was concluded that the finds were probably works from the fifth century. They could have been robbers' loot which were buried in a hurry.

Before being concealed the objects - 160 articles in all - had been crushed or flattened into a heap of metal. It took painstaking and difficult restoration to return them to their original shapes. The items can be perhaps counted as amongst the most precious which are on display today at the National Museum of Antiquities, Queen Street, Edinburgh.

Secret of the Prentice Pillar

Visitors to historic Rosslyn Chapel seldom fail to be impressed by the beautifully carved Apprentice Pillar which stands eight feet high and is situated close to the entrance of the Crypt. But behind its creation lies a grim story of murder.

According to legend a master mason was given a model of a pillar which could be seen in Rome. The plan was to create a replica at Rosslyn. The mason had a great deal of enthusiasm for the project and to ensure that the job would be perfect he decided to travel over to the continent and study the original at first hand. During this trip his apprentice hit on the idea of carving the pillar as a surprise for the mason. The young lad was only trying to please his master but in the process he created a fascinating work of art which is first class in every detail. Unfortunately instead of being pleased upon his return the mason flew into a jealous rage and smashed the lad over the head with a mallet. The young genius died on the spot.

A short time afterwards the Chapel had to be reconsecrated 'after some dreadful act.' It is most likely that this was the murder of the apprentice. In the roof of the chapel is a head with a scar on the right temple. This is thought to be a carving of the apprentice. In the opposite corner is a head of the master mason. A third head is said to represent the boy's mother. It is thought that these heads were carved by the workmen when the walls had reached that height in order to symbolise the story.

Without doubt the Apprentice Pillar is unlike any of the others in the chapel. It has a style and quality which people have marvelled at for generations. At the base of the pillar are the symbols of Satan - eight dragons intertwined.

The Faeries' Cradle

Our forefathers believed that the fairies took great delight in stealing newly born infants from the cradle and leaving mischievous changelings in their place. All sorts of customs and rites were adopted to try and stop this happening.

But even if the wee folk managed to beat such measures and take the child, distraught parents could always find hope at St. Bennet's Spring near Cromarty. For by passing the changeling through a trough of water there the imposter immediately vanished and their snatched child would be restored to them. The trough, known as "Fairies' Cradle" had a sudden end in 1745 when the parish minister and two elders broke it to pieces so that "it might no longer serve the purposes of superstition."

River Spirits

In the minds of our ancestors the link between water and magic did not end at wells. Each river was believed to have its own guardian spirit which was capable of transforming itself into shapes familiar to man. Most spirits appeared as horses and when in this form were known as "kelpies." Everyone knew, of course, that a river needed to have several victims through drowning every so often if it was to remain happy so to satisfy its thirst the kelpie would meet up with a weary foot traveller. No opposition would be offered when the inevitable attempt was made at a mount. Once the unsuspecting victim was safely aboard there was no way he could get off. The kelpie then went galloping off to the river and promptly deposited his prey into the swirling waters. The River Spey's spirit when in kelpie form appeared to the innocent onlooker as a beautiful white horse.

Spirits could also take on the appearance of people. That of the River Conon in Ross-shire used to appear "as a tall woman dressed in green, but distinguished chiefly by her withered meagre countenance, forever distorted by a malignant scowl." She was one of the most hostile spirits of all.

The tradition that rivers needed a victim from time to time to satisfy the spirit's thirst is noted in the following well-known rhyme:-

Blood-thirsty Dee
Each year needs three;
But bonny Don
She needes none.

There were times when the spirits did give help. After a basket-maker by the name of Farquharson drowned in the Dee his body could not be found. When the final searches were called off his widow took along the man's plaid, knelt down by the water's side, and prayed to the river to give her the corpse back. She then threw the plaid into the Dee. Next morning Farquharson was found. Wrapped around him was the plaid.

A similar story is recorded of the Don at Inverurie. Relatives anxious to recover the drowned body of a loved one were told by an old woman to place a biscuit in the water at the point where he met his end. They were then to follow its progress. The body would be found at the point where the biscuit sank. They followed her instructions carefully and it worked!

Lochs had spirits which made demands on inhabitants. The first lamb of the flock from several local farms had to be drowned in a small loch on the Aberdeenshire/Banffshire boundary. Any farmer who didn't keep his side of the bargain would find half of his sheep drowned before the close of the grazing season.

Lady Agnes snatched it from his hand

Revenge of a Poisoned Girl

An intriguing story lies behind the reported sighting once a year of a female phantom who rises from the site of the old castle of Leys and glides over the Hill of Banchory to Crathes Castle. It takes us back some four hundred years when the castle on the Loch of Leys was occupied by Lady Agnes, a proud independent widow and her son Alexander. When the boy was 17 they had a visit from a French relative named Sir Roger de Bernard. He had brought his daughter Bertha to Scotland for safe-keeping while he returned home to sort out his problems. Alexander and Bertha got on very well together and passed the days riding over the moors and visiting friends. Soon they were head over heels in love and everyone was delighted.

Everyone that is except Lady Agnes. She wanted her son to marry into the noble family of the Lords of Lorne. Alexander, however, was determined to ignore her disapproval. Then Lady Agnes hit on a drastic solution. While her son was away on business at Arbroath she poisoned their young guest with 'doctored' wine. Alexander returned home to find Bertha lying in the centre of the castle's main room on a bier.

Overcome with shock he went to sip some wine from a nearby goblet but Lady Agnes snatched it from his hand and threw the contents into the loch. Their eyes met and Alexander, horrified, realised what she had done. He loved Bertha yet at the same time couldn't bring himself to turn his own mother over to the authorities.

Some twelve months later while they were eating supper Sir Roger de Bernard arrived. News had recently reached him about Bertha's death and he accused Lady Agnes of murdering the girl. As he spoke the room turned very chilly and objects started moving about of their own accord. Then the widow was suddenly jolted upwards in her chair. Slowly she got to her feet screaming: "She comes, she comes." A few seconds later Lady Agnes was on the floor. . .dead.

Justice had been done. Alexander eventually married Janet Hamilton, kinswoman of Archbishop Hamilton. They decided that the old building would be best left to its sad memories and in 1533 work was started on construction of the present Crathes Castle.

Magic Wells

In times past almost every parish in the North-East had a well which was said to possess remarkable qualities for healing this or that ailment. Our forefathers firmly believed in the reputations which had built up around certain waters and in search of a cure they ran the risk of heavy fines and humiliating public rebukes from the churches.

Christian teachers frowned upon the faith which folk placed in wells and kirk sessions, anxious to stamp out the primitive beliefs, imposed stiff penalties on those who were caught ignoring their instructions not to visit wells for the purposes of healing.

However they could not stop the steady procession of sick men and women or relatives who made pilgrimages to places like the chapel well of St. Mary's in the old parish of Dundurcus on Speyside. Its water had been famed from time immemorial as a great health giver and for 200 years after the Reformation the weak came, from Buchan in the east to the Hebrides in the west, to quench their thirsts.

Elgin parish records of the late sixteenth and much of the seventeenth centuries contain details of steps taken to deal with offenders. One man lost his job as a church official and others were fined for visiting St. Mary's. Still more pilgrims had to go through the mental agony of a verbal roasting in front of the congregation.

St. Fittack's Well, near the old church of St. Fittack's at the Bay of Nigg, south of Aberdeen, was a favourite with folk who wanted to improve their overall health by drinking the cool water. From the Reformation onwards the church tried to put an end to the visits and the kirk session of the burgh made it an offence to go to St. Fittack's "in ane superstitious manner." The town council gave their backing on May 16, 1616. A maximum £2 fine would be imposed on all heads of families, wives or children found guilty of breaking the ban. For servants the maximum penalty would be £1 payable by employers who in law were responsible for them.

Some of the cures claimed by particular wells were interesting. Whooping cough vanished instantly after a visit to a fountain near the burn of Oxhill in Rathven while the Fuaran Fiountag at Strathspey cured toothache. Skin disease or sores were helped at Fergan's Well, Kirkmichael, Banffshire. The best times for visiting most wells were reckoned to be the first Sundays of November, February, May and August.

Wells of Health

In centuries past a curious ceremony was performed at a well in Livingston which stood in the grounds of the Royal hunting lodge. At sunrise of New Year's Day folk, who had collected some of its precious liquid, would queue up to be blessed and touched by the king. If they suffered from conditions such as skin disease they were sure to be completely cured within the coming year.

One explanation of this custom could be that many skin conditions are caused through nervous disorders. A blessing by the king could have convinced people in their minds that they were better mentally thus leaving nature to do the rest. It was also established some 600 years later that the well produced more of a thin oil which flowed from the shale rock below the surface rather than water. This would obviously have been better for bad skin compared with the ordinary water which folk probably used prior to their visit.

Whitekirk, East Lothian, had a well many centuries ago which was given the credit of curing a variety of diseases. An old Vatican document traces its origins to the victory of Edward I of England over the Scots at Dunbar in 1294. Some of the defeated soldiers took refuge in Dunbar Castle which was then in the possession of Black Agnes. Later she tried to escape but was injured and forced to come ashore at Fairknowe. There Agnes drank from a well and made an instant recovery.

The Countess was very impressed by this and later created a chapel beside the well. However as the siege of Dunbar happened some 40 years later we must doubt the accuracy of at least some parts of the document.

What is certain is that tens of thousands of people visited the well. James I built extensions to the chapel and called it White Chapel. Finally, according to the document, the lands and possessions of the chapel were seized during the Reformation. the reformers "beat the shrine to pieces." the chapel was made a parish church and became known as Whitekirk.

On Soutra Hill there was once a hospital which Malcolm IV had built in the 1160s for the reception of travellers. A short distance below the site of the hospital - almost all trace of which vanished more than 140 years ago - was a gathering spot for sick folk from all over the Lothians. There they would drink from the Trinity Well which was said to cure a number of conditions.

Invaders Hid in Hay Cart

Edward I of England was feared up and down the country as The Hammer of the Scots. During his invasion of Scotland in the first years of the fourteenth century he fortified Linlithgow Palace and stayed there during the winters of 1301 and 1302.

Unfortunately his son and successor, Edward II, wasn't as crafty or as wise as dad. He lost control of the Palace after being outwitted by an old Linlithgow farmer called Binnie.

It seems that Binnie had an order to make a weekly delivery of hay for the English horses. He was a fairly simple country fellow, somewhat slow of movement and anything but the brightest of souls. His snail pace manner regularly brought jeers from the English garrison but as a resident of the fair toun might have later remarked, 'They didnae ken that auld Binnie was onythin' but daft.' For the invaders got the biggest shock of their lives when Binnie made his weekly delivery of hay and as usual was allowed to pass them without the cart's contents being checked - for out jumped 12 Scottish soldiers! They were backed up by other men who were hiding nearby and after a struggle gained control of the Palace.

Unfortunately Robert the Bruce didn't have enough men to spare for defence of the Palace so he had to have it burned down thus depriving the enemy of the chance to use it again as a strategic base.

Later the Palace was of course rebuilt and it was from there in 1513, that King James IV left to fight - and die - on Flodden Field. The night before he had gone to pray at St. Michael's Church. As he spoke to God "ane figure of ane blue coated man" appeared out of thin air and warned of the disaster that lay ahead. James chose to ignore the apparition and later died in the mud of the battlefield - his country defeated and broken.

Miracle Vision

A King's encounter with a killer stag led to the foundation of Holyrood Abbey in the twelfth century.

The story began on the morning of a Holy Rood Day - September 14. David I was staying at Edinburgh Castle and although the day was an important religious festival he ignored pleas from his churchmen to spend the time in prayer and holy worship. . .preferring instead to go on a hunting trip.

The king loved the thrill of the chase and one of his favourite sporting grounds was Drumsheugh Forest. Today the area is a busy commercial centre but in his time the thick woodlands were full of deer, foxes and many other members of the animal kingdom.

So it was a jolly party which the king led out of the castle on that autumn morning so long ago. A chase was soon underway after the footservants had spotted a young deer and forced it to flee.

But during the hunt David became separated from his companions. He carried on alone for a while then stopped to have a drink of water from a spring. He was bending down to quench his thirst by the pool's edge when the peace around him was broken by a loud noise coming from the surrounding bushes.

Then a giant stag appeared before the defenceless king. The beast attacked and its antlers pinned him to the ground.

He seemed doomed to die. . .until a little silver cloud appeared in the sky. As the stag was about to move in for the kill a vision of the cross came from within the cloud. At this the animal reared backwards, turned and fled.

David was naturally in a state of severe shock and it took every ounce of energy he could muster to crawl through the trees in search of his horse. He found it a few minutes later and sounded a call on his horn. This summoned his fellow hunters and when the king told them of his encounter they were dumbfounded.

The king decided to do something as a tribute to God for saving his life. Then later that night St. Andrew, Patron Saint of Scotland, appeared at his bedside. David was told to build a church and monastery on the spot where his life had been saved.

The order was of course obeyed and a great clearing was made in the forest. No cost or effort was spared in building an impressive Abbey which was dedicated to the Holy Rood. (i.e. cross).

Other buildings were added later and Augustinian monks from St. Andrews settled there.

The king made sure that they would never want for anything. Gifts of land in various parts of Scotland together with forestry, fishing and grazing rights in other areas helped to make Holyrood prosperous. Examples of the perks included: half of the fishing in Inverleith Harbour; the right to fish for salmon and herring in the Clyde; free grazing for their swine in Stirlingshire Forest and unlimited supplies of timber from the same area free of charge.

They were also of course allowed to create their own town outside the Abbey walls over which they had complete control.

The monks also operated a sanctuary and Arthur's Seat as well as the Holyrood Park we know today fell within its boundaries. Whilst inside a fellow was safe from his creditors for 24 hours. Apparently at the end of this period the debtor had to apply to the Abbey for permission to leave the park without fear of being hounded further.

There are of course historians who will tell us that the incident of the vision was pure invention. The monks devised the story to win more gifts for their order they will say. However nothing is ever. . .absolutely certain. . .

Murder at the Manse

Murder at the Manse

An East Lothian parish minister cold bloodedly murdered his wife as the church bells were ringing for him to take Sunday morning service - then he faked the death scene to give the impression that she had committed suicide by hanging herself.

Later, after delivering what was said to be one of his best sermons, the Rev. John Kello of Spott invited some friends back to the manse for lunch so that his wife, Margaret, would have company. The minister explained that she had been very depressed and went on to stun his parishioners by suggesting that the Devil through local witches was attempting to possess her soul. The luncheon guests expressed their concern and sympathy to Mr Kello as they strolled round to the manse. He nodded and sighed sadly. One could only hope through the power of prayer that the forces of good would overcome those of evil!

Before leaving for the service the preacher had locked all the doors of the manse and slipped out through an exit from his study which was never used from one year's end to the next. And when the guests found the place locked up he gave another dazzling display of acting. What on earth could be wrong? What has happened to my wife?

Eventually Mr Kello got in through a window which was slightly open. Seconds later guests heard him cry: "Oh, my wife, my wife, my beloved wife is gone!"

He opened the door to let them in. Mrs Kello was hanging on a rope suspended from a rafter. The visitors began to speculate on the forces of evil which must have driven the lady of the manse, a simple kind hearted country soul, to commit such an unpardonable sin while her poor husband preached from the pulpit. By nightfall the news was round the entire district and many an old woman had been branded by her neighbours as a hag who was in league with Satan to destroy the Christian folk of Spott.

Only Mr Kello knew the real truth of how his wife died. How he had gone into her room as she was getting dressed for service and put a towel round her neck. How he had pulled it tighter and tighter ignoring her pathetic cries to stop. How he had then used rope from the bleaching green to hang the corpse. How an earlier attempt to poison her with an overdose of drugs failed.

This man of God, who 10 years before, had been passed by John Knox and commissioners sitting in Edinburgh as being "maist qualified for the ministering of the Word of God and sacraments and reiding of the Common prayer publicklie in all kirks and congregations," didn't even stop to consider their three children. In fact he had happily sent the youngsters - Bartilmo, Barbara and Bessie - to another county manse for a week's holiday so that the field would be clear for murder.

His motive was greed. Land investments weren't bringing in a return and he found life on a minister's wage very difficult. It was no secret that one or two wealthy ladies of the area were greatly impressed by his style and use of words. With Margaret out of the way he would be free to marry money and live comfortably ever after.

However this was not to be. After that fateful day Kello found it impossible to sleep properly. In the stillness of the night when the only sound was the rustling of trees outside his bedroom window he could hear his victim call out from beyond the grave. When Kello did doze off he always had the same nightmare but before long was jolted back to reality his face and body a mass of sweat.

At the time the minister in Dunbar was the Rev. Andrew Simpson, a brilliant scholar and a noted psychic. Kello explained the nightmare to him. . .

"Methought a great man came and carried me by force before the face of ane terrible judge and to escape his fury I did precipitate myself in ane deep river. But there was for me no escape. For even in the depths of the rushing river did his angels and messengers follow me; and with two-edged swords they struck at me and swore as they struck.

"Siccan a terror was mine that I did decline and jouk in the water, and mony a time strack at me as I joukit, and aye mine end seemed surely come, and yet again wad I jouk, though the stream ran fierce, in a spate, till in the end, by ane way unknown to me, I did escape."

Mr Simpson gave him a frank interpretation of the nightmare. The Great Man who called him before God was his own conscience. The messengers of God were the processes of law and order. The water was his own vain hypocrisy and blasphemy. The minister went on: "Your deliverance shall be spiritual. God shall pull you from the grip of Satan and make you confess."

Kello did confess and a few weeks later, in October, 1570, a large crowd saw him hang in the Grassmarket, Edinburgh. Afterwards, on the instructions of the court, his corpse was burned. All the preacher's possessions and the land he owned were forfeited to the authorities. But later these were returned to the unfortunate orphans one of whom went on to become a minister.

Secret of Jack the Runner

Glamis Castle, near Kirriemuir, is linked with several ghost stories and other eerie happenings.

But its biggest concerns a monster said to have been kept prisoner in a hidden chamber because of his hideous appearance. According to legend he was the first son of one of the Earls and was born with an abnormally large head.

It was thought that the baby wouldn't last for long and his parents refused to have anything to do with him. But the monster survived and lived to reach the age of 50. During walks for exercise the unwanted son tried to escape from the confines of the battlements. On several occasions he was seen, it is claimed, running across the lawns of the castle and around the outskirts of the village of Glamis. The creature made strange noises and locals nicknamed him Jack the Runner.

In the nineteenth century tradesmen working at Glamis came across a tunnel in the walls. Not long afterwards those who made the discovery suddenly emigrated with their wives and children.

Four servants, who were murdered in an upper room after being caught drinking and gambling, are said to return once a year. Their terrifying screams are heard as the slaughter is re-enacted.

Another phantom is a fellow by the name of Beardie. During the course of the present century there have been reports of guests' encounters with him. He is thought to be a Scottish nobleman who was killed during a fight at the castle in the sixteenth century.

The Grey Lady has been spotted on many occasions kneeling and praying in different parts of Glamis. The spirit of a young girl makes appearances in the Royal apartments.

Even before it was created Glamis was at the centre of a mystery - apparently it was to be built on a hill. The foundations were laid but when the workmen arrived each morning they found that the stones cut and laid the previous day had been smashed and scattered during the night.

The family concluded that they were victims of mischief by the fairies and not wishing to antogonise the Little Folk, removed the site to flat land in the valley of Strathmore.

The oldest part of the castle is the fifteenth century tower. It was from here that a widowed Lady Glamis was taken for burning at the stake.

Mob stole Dead Royals

Bones of the dead were stolen from their coffins and scattered on the ground by an angry Edinburgh mob. They were on the warpath over a decision by King James VII to turn the abbey church at Holyrood into a place of catholic worship.

James, who was a devout Roman Catholic, made his declaration after coming to the throne in 1685.

But things were to change when he was later forced to give up the crown and go abroad after the thrones of England and Scotland were offered to William and Mary of Orange.

The Duke of Gordon continued to hold the Palace for James and ignored a command from the Privy Council to get out. Eventually the City guard managed to gain access through the back and forced him to surrender.

It was after this that the mob moved in. In the king's private chapel books, ornaments and vestments were destroyed. The Chapel Royal, their next target, was left a complete ruin.

Then the Royal Vault was broken into. Lids were ripped off coffins and the bones were scattered all over the place.

As it happens an inspection of the bodies in the coffins had been made a few years before this dreadful raid so it was possible to know whose bones were disturbed.

A report of the inspection mentions "King James ye fyft of Scotland," Queen Mary's father, whose body was measured as being well over seven feet.

Other coffins contained the remains of Magdalene of France, Prince Arthur, third son of James IV, Arthur, Duke of Albany, second son of James VI, Lord Darnley and a Countess of Argyle.

In 1898 Queen Victoria had as many of these remains as possible collected and placed in one large coffin in the Chapel Royal with the inscription giving the names of those who had been removed. The list includes David II and James II who were taken into the Chapel Royal from the Abbey Church after it had been destroyed.

Devil Coach

In the seventeenth century James Carnegie, second Earl of Southesk, studied the secrets of black magic at Padua and according to legend the Devil was one of his teachers. Lessons were free but Auld Nick's reward was the soul of a pupil who happened to be last out of the class on a particular day.

James was unlucky enough to end up as the victim but, thanks to a bit of fast talking, was able to persuade the Devil to accept his shadow instead. From that day on he had to go through life with no shadow and tried to walk in the shade as much as possible and thus not look too out of the ordinary.

It seems, however, that the Devil did get Carnegie's soul in the end. Tradition states that on the day of the Earl's death in the Brechin district in 1669 Auld Nick came to collect him in a coach which was drawn by six black horses. This thundered off into the night and then plunged down a well near the family burial ground.

After that night many Forfarshire folk claimed to have seen the devil coach repeat its deathly runs at certain times of the year.

A Troubled Family

After retiring from a successful retail business in the Borders Mr William Whittingen moved his wife and family of five to a large detached house which stood on the outskirts of Perth. He had been able to buy it for a knockdown price from a family who were willing to sell cheap for ready cash.

But before long the Whittingens ended up wishing that they had never set eyes on the house. For it claimed three of their lives and landed one in an asylum for the criminally insane following three incidents involving the appearances of ghosts.

Daughter Mary was the first victim. She had gone to her room to pick up some photographs which a guest wanted to see. While she was looking for them the phantom of a piper, wearing a kilt, materialised and stared at her. Not surprisingly the poor girl was overcome with shock and a subsequent check with the servants confirmed that no strangers had been allowed to enter the house. Exactly one week after this incident Mary was seriously injured after tripping over a hoop which had been left on the croquet lawn. During the fall a hatpin went through her head.

This led to her blood being poisoned and a few days later she was dead.

Tragedy number two came the following Christmas. A coach full of phantoms thundered up the driveway and screeched to a halt at the front door. The weird crew on board then entered the house and stared for a while at daughter Ruth. She fainted in terror and on recovering after the spirits had departed the poor girl declared that she was doomed to die just like her sister. A fortnight later appendicitis struck her. Peritonitis set in and she died on the operating table.

The third, and final death, came over a year later. Son Ernest, his wife and baby were house guests. Martha, the third daughter, doted on the child but one day the evil piper appeared, took possession of her soul, and made her cut the baby's throat with a pair of scissors. Once the murder had been completed he began playing a dirge and then vanished through the window. This restored Martha to her former self. The realisation that she had committed murder made her hysterical and everyone in the house ran to the room. Of course the story of the ghost was put down to something else and she was committed to a criminal lunatic asylum.

Soon afterwards the house was sold. It was then demolished and a new building was erected on the spot.

Naughty Monks Burned Alive!

Besides spreading the word of Christianity the monks of Newbattle
Abbey were noted for their pioneering work in the field of coal-mining
and agriculture. But not all of the white-robed fathers were as dedicated
as history might have us believe. . .

Our story concerns two monks who were burned to death by an irate
father because of love affairs they were carrying on with local women! It
all happened in 1375. Then the lands of the Gilmerton district belonged
to Sir John Heron, or Herring, a distinguished knight of the day who had
fought in many bloody conflicts against the English. He had two
daughters and planned that the eldest, Margaret, should marry his
brother's son. After the wedding they would be made heirs to the greater
part of the estate. But complications arose when Margaret became
romantically involved with a monk from Newbattle Abbey. She was a
deeply religious girl and frequently made the three mile journey to
worship there. The monk was quick to see that Sir John's daughter was
something of an innocent at large and a short time after their first
meeting he seduced her. They began to have regular meetings at a little
farm called the Grange which stood just outside Gilmerton. Their
secret was safe enough with the widow who owned the farm. She was
having an affair with another monk!

However through time rumours of the illicit goings-on at the Grange
reached Sir John's ears and he banned his daughter from going there.
She promised to obey the instruction but that very night sneaked out of
the house and made for the farm where her lover was waiting. Before
retiring to his bed Sir John decided to make a check in his daughter's
room and got quite a shock when he discovered that she wasn't there.
Absolutely furious he summoned two servants and they all made for the
Grange. He banged on the door and shouted on his daughter to come
out but not a sound came from within the house. Still in a very angry
mood the irate father took a torch from the hands of one of the servants
and set fire to the thatch. A high wind was blowing and the flames
spread rapidly. The house was soon a mass of flames and its nine
occupants, including the two monks and Margaret, met a horrific death.

For this cruel act Sir John had to flee the country and his estate was
forfeited to the king. The murder of the two monks was condemned as
sacrilege. Sir Walter Somerville, a good friend, tried to win him a
pardon. He protested to the Abbot of Newbattle about the immoral
lives which the monks had apparently been living for years. Eventually
after much wheeling and dealing a settlement was agreed on the
following lines. . .

"That Sir John should make over the merk land of the Grange, where the murder was committed, to, and in favour of the Abbey of Newbattle, claiming no right therein, neither in property, superiority etc. . .and, further, that the said Sir John should, bareheaded and barelegged, in sackcloth, crave absolution at the Bishop and Abbot's hands, and stand in the same manner at the principal door of St. Catherine's Chapel every Sabbath and holy day for one year, and paying forty pennies at every time to the poor of the parish, and one hundred merks Scots to the monks of Newbattle to pray for the souls of those that died through his transgression."

The Troubled Servant

Supernatural disturbances at a house near Aberdeen's Great Western Road ended abruptly with the discovery under floorboards of an envelope containing a postal order. The place had been empty for some time and a Mr Scarfe, who took a keen interest in things not of this world, was interested to hear of the ghostly goings-on while staying with some friends in the Granite City. He decided to find out more by spending a night there.

During the course of the evening the spirit of a servant girl appeared before him. She signalled Mr Scarfe to follow, then glided up the stairs. Needless to say he was terribly nervous but managed to stay cool. In the garret the ghost stopped at the hearth, pointed downwards for a few seconds then vanished into thin air.

Scarfe stayed just long enough to mark the spot. Next day he returned with the landlord who tore up the floorboards. All they found was a letter. At first it didn't appear to be anything of particular interest but as the two made further enquiries, an incredible story was unfolded.

They established that a few years earlier the house had been occupied by a fairly prosperous trades family who employed a servant girl called Anna Webb. Her description exactly fitted that of the ghost seen by Mr Scarfe. One morning Anna had been given some letters to post by the lady of the house but one containing a postal order never reached its destination. She was suspected of theft and threatened with prosecution. A continual barrage of questions from her employers drove Anna, a nervous lassie, to suicide.

At a subsequent inquiry into her death a note which she had written was produced. It stated: "As proof of my innocence I am going to hang myself. I never stole your letter and can only suppose it was lost in the post."

The discovery of the unopened letter would seem to suggest that Anna was completely innocent and the disturbances at the house finished the day those floorboards were lifted.

Dig, Willie, and Drink!

A voice came back from the dead, helped cure a young man of a terminal disease, and made a well near Cromarty famous as a watering-hole where the sick could go and be cured. The well became known as Fiddler's Well after William Fiddler made a miraculous recovery from consumption. He and a friend had been seized by the condition at the same time. The second young man died soon afterwards and William, who by now was wasted away to a shadow, needed every ounce of strength he could muster to attend the funeral.

That night he had great difficulty in getting to sleep. The loss of his best pal and the pain within his own body combined to make rest very difficult. It was only after many hours of tossing and turning that he eventually fell into a deep sleep. The peace was broken by a dream in which his departed companion asked William to go to a spot on the outskirts of the town. William arose from his bed, still sleeping, and walked there. At the appointed rendezvous he sat down and a few minutes later a bee started buzzing around his head. The buzzing seemed to take on the voice of his dead companion and it was saying: "Dig, Willie, and drink! Dig, Willie, and drink!"

William obeyed the command and no sooner had he torn the first sod than a spring of clear water gushed from the hollow. Next day he returned to the spot - this time wide awake - and drank from the spring. It restored him to full health.

Hugh Miller in "Scenes and Legends of the North of Scotland," a most fascinating old book, says: "Its virtues are still celebrated, for though the water be only simple water it must be drank in the morning, and as it gushes from the bank; and, with pure air, exercise and early rising for its auxiliaries it continues to work cures."

The Masked Hangman

A hangman who took cold feet a short time before he was due to carry out the death penalty sparked off a spectacular mystery in Dundee. For a volunteer came forward for the job and only made one stipulation to the junior bailie who was in charge of the proceedings. . .'Let me wear a mask.'

At that time executions were great public occasions and on the day of Saturday May 30, 1835, folk poured into the city from the surrounding countryside to see the hanging of Mark Devlin. He was a young Irish born hand-loom weaver who had come to Scotland six years earlier and found work in Glasgow. In 1832 he moved to Dundee and rented a house in the Hilltown. Crime and muggings were a serious problem which the police force of 14 constables were impotent to tackle.

Devlin soon fell into bad company and on February 29, 1835, was arrested with two other men in connection with housebreaking. Later the more serious charge of assault on a 14-year-old girl was brought against him. In May he was found guilty of this at Perth Circuit Court and sentenced to be hanged.

An executioner, probably from either Glasgow or Edinburgh, was brought in to carry out the death penalty but no clear explanation was ever given as to why he suddenly withdrew.

After the masked hangman had sent Devlin into eternity rumours began that he was a fellow by the name of James Livingstone. . .a showman who travelled round Scotland with hobby-horses and merry-go-rounds.

The widespread talk prompted Mr Livingston to send a letter to the Dundee Advertiser in which he stated: "You are aware that the individual who acted as hangman at the execution of Mark Devlin did so in disguise. Some malicious enemy has circulated a report that I was the individual; and I have been openly assailed with the false accusation.

"On the day of the execution I was in Forfar market (this statement is confirmed by an adjacent letter signed by the provost and two bailies of that town). . .Perhaps I have not any right to call upon the Magistrates of Dundee for the name of the individual; but I publicly call upon the presiding Magistrate to exonerate me. I am a poor man with a family, and cannot afford to lose my character in such a manner."

As it happened the Dundee Magistrates never responded to the appeal. All who knew the identity of the masked hangman took their secret to the grave. . .

Lesson from a Ghost

Gamekeeper James Macfarlane was a real ladies man. He was always chasing the girls and frequently ignored his employer's orders that all servants should attend a Sunday evening gathering for family prayers.

However James, from Callander, suddenly changed his ways one night and became a deeply religious man.

The reason for this transformation - considered by friends as 'incredible' - was a meeting with the ghost of his dead master at Cambusmore.

It all started at one of the Sunday prayer meetings when the master condemned James in front of the assembled gathering and vowed to give him a fright that would make him mend his ways on the Sabbath.

Later that night the old man collapsed and died in his bedroom. At the precise time of death the gamekeeper returning from a date in Doune, stumbled across his boss lying in the path that led to Cambusmore.

He was shocked to see the face of his master but on examining the body he could feel nothing. The poor gamie ran off in terror as he realised that he was trying to revive a ghost.

His worst fears were confirmed when he got back to the big house and was told of the master's death.

From that night James was a changed man. He never dated a girl on a Sunday, went to church regularly and said his prayers every morning and evening. To those who mocked his belief in ghosts James would say: "I ken weel what I hae seen ma'sel."

Green Lady Riddle

Since Pictish times there has been a military base on the hill which today houses Stirling Castle and down through history this site has witnessed many bloody deaths. So it is not surprising that the Castle is rich in stories of ghosts and supernatural happenings.

The most baffling spirit to grace its corridors and chambers is the moaning Green Lady. Who is she?

One theory is that our phantom friend was a Royal maidservant who made her name by saving the life of Mary Queen of Scots.

Mary, who some years earlier had been warned that her life would be put in danger by fire at Stirling Castle, was sound asleep when the maid walked in to find her bed on fire. Minutes later the Queen would have been burned beyond recognition but the quick thinking girl dragged her clear as the flames spread.

Another theory names the Green Lady as the spirit of a pretty teenager who died of a broken heart after her soldier fiance was mistakenly killed by a flying arrow while on sentry duty.

In recent times a cook, busy making dinner, collapsed after seeing her. While stirring the soup he felt a chill at his back and sensed he was being watched. The cook turned round to see the Green Lady watching his preparations with extreme interest.

Phantom footsteps of a sentry who is understood to have met a terrible death in the early 19th century - "struck down by some dark sperrit or demon" - have been heard at the Governor's Block.

His face had a look of absolute fear which sent chills down the spine of all those who saw the body before the funeral.

Later soldiers refused to patrol the area where their comrade had been found dead and disciplinary action was taken against them.

The Body Snatchers

In the earlier years of the 19th century doctors found it very difficult to get bodies for research because of the public's attitude to human dissection so they gladly paid out huge sums of money to folk who could keep them supplied. Most corpses found their way to the anatomist's table after being stolen from the grave and the medical men, usually folk of high principle, never asked any questions.

A dark cloudy night with no moon or an evening of torrential rain were ideal conditions for the bodysnatchers or "Resurrectionists" as these traders in human corpses were known.

In 1822 the beadle of Stirling's West Church noticed one morning that the grave of a woman called Witherspoon had been disturbed. Later Bailie Jaffrey, who had a grocery store in Baker Street, gave orders that the grave was to be opened. The body had vanished from the coffin and the shroud and dead-clothes were huddled together at one end of the grave.

No-one was ever caught for this outrage, but at the Spring Circuit Court of 1822 a grave-digger and some others were tried on a charge of lifting bodies from Stirling Churchyard.

They claimed the orders to steal the bodies had been given by a doctor but he left the town before proceedings could be taken against him.

The citizens, bitter about the activities of the despicable bodysnatchers, rioted during the trial and the 77th Regiment had to be drafted in to calm the mob. They fired over the heads of the crowd. No one was injured.

To counter the activities of Resurrectionists, who were seldom caught, families had their nearest and dearest buried with an iron cage secured around the coffin. This was kept there until the body was past being of use to doctors.

However it was only when the law made provision for medics to be supplied with specimens that the problem was finally eased.

Wolf on the Crag

A wolf once saved Stirling from destruction and the townsfolk from certain death. In the ninth century two Northumbrian princes, named Osbrecht and Ella, seized much of East and Central Scotland from Donald V, King of Scots. Stirling was one of their strongholds and was guarded by scores of soldiers.

But soon they were under attack and efforts were made to take the town from them just as they had seized it from the Scots. I use the word town but of course in those times Stirling was a village of just a few hundred inhabitants who lived in wooden houses built beside the fortress. Nevertheless this was an important place and our two Northumbrian princes did all they could to protect it from a threatened invasion by the Danes who had earlier brought terror to many towns in Britain.

At a crag on the southern side of town a sentry was posted to keep watch round the clock. But one of the soldiers involved in this task fell asleep on duty. . .and it was on the very night that the enemy was poised to attack.

In that fascinating old book "The Stirling Repository" we are told: "The besieging foe was at hand, and was about to take the city, when a wolf, alarmed at the noise and din of the advancing hordes, crept for safety to the crag on which the sleeping soldier lay.

"But still he found no safety. He growled in terror. It was his wild cry that saved the city. It awoke the sleeping sentinel, who, seeing the position of matters, raised the alarm.

"He was not yet too late. The citizens arose, buckled on their armour, and drove the Danes from the district. Thus the wolf saved the city."

Later the seal of the burgh became a wolf recumbent on a crag and those who asked about the origin of the design were told this story.

Facts do exist to back up the yarn. For a start wolves were reported in the area. In 1288 the accounts record an allowance "for two park-keepers and one hunter of wolves at Stirling." In the 15th century wolves were condemned in Scotland as "pests."

The Glowing Hand

King Robert the Bruce knew that he would win the battle of Bannockburn in 1314 - before the fighting had even started! And it was all thanks to a phantom monk.

Robert had ordered a priest to bring the glowing hand of the holy Saint Fillan from Stirling Castle to the battlefield. The Lord had made the hand give off bright light so that Saint Fillan could work long into the night while writing out the Holy Scriptures.

The king was convinced that the presence of the hand would bring Scotland good luck in the confrontation that lay ahead.

However the priest, fearing that the hand might be lost to the English, hid it in one of the castle dungeons and brought the empty box to Bannockburn. He anticipated that Robert wouldn't ask to see inside. . .but was wrong.

"Let me look at the hand," said his king and, trembling with fear, the priest slowly lifted the top off. By a miracle the glowing hand was inside. However, standing opposite, and only visible to the priest, was a stern faced monk dressed in a long white gown. He warned the Royal messenger: "Never again must you disobey your King."

The father broke down and confessed all to Robert. He expected to be cruelly punished for disobeying such an important order but the king simply smiled and said a short prayer. For he knew this was an omen that his side would score an important victory in the fighting.

And, as every schoolboy knows, Scotland were indeed victorious at Bannockburn.

Dead Man's Fury

Stirling farmer Allan Mair was a white haired old man - hated and despised by everyone for miles around. He lost most of his money raising trespass actions against folk and frequently beat up his wife until her body was bruised black and blue.

But fate took a hand in the cruel and evil life of this villain on Sunday May 14, 1843. Neighbours heard Mrs Mair, a soul of some 84 summers, screaming with pain as she went through the ordeal of another thrashing. But suddenly the cries turned to weak groans and those forced to listen remarked: "There's dathe in the auld body's cup noo."

The police were called and Mair was arrested protesting his innocence. Asked for a plea he told Lord Moncrieff at the Circuit Court on September 19: "I'm no' guilty; It wasna me that did it, as true's Goad's in heaven! It was Sandy Nimmo that cam' in at the bole and did it! Noo, that's as true as ye are there ma' lord."

However the jury unanimously found him guilty of murder and the execution was arranged for October 4.

On the morning that the death sentence was to be passed Mair spoke in his cell to the Rev. Mr Stark as crowds gathered in the streets to watch the hanging.

"How do you feel?" asked the minister.

"Feel sir! I canna tell ye hoo I feel! I canna think that in twa 'oors' time I'll be lying on the braid o' my back a deid man! Oh sir! I suppose nae paurdon has come? Sadly the minister confirmed that no reprieve had been granted.

Later in a dramatic outburst from the gallows Mair shouted at his fellow citizens: "I've no been given an opportunity to prove that my innocence was as clear as the noon-day sun! the minister o' the parish invented lees - lees against me!

"The constable that took me wudna alloo me to bring awa' papers frae my hoose which micht ha'e spoken in my favour. The Fiscal and Sheriff in Fa'kirk prevented me frae proving my innocence.

"They wudna alloo me to bring witnesses wha could easily ha'e cleared me frae the crime wi' which I am unjustly charged, and as unjustly condemned.

"They wudna even alloo me to write a bit letter to thae witnesses, and I declare that for thae reasons I am quite certain that Goad frae heevin' will rain doon fire and brimstane upon them and destroy them!

"Folks I'm nae murderer. I say again I was condemned by the lees o' the minister, by the injustice o' a sheriff and fiscal, and by the perjury of the witnesses. I curse them a'."

The crowd were unimpressed and called out to the hangman: 'Dispatch him!' 'Awa wi' him,' and 'Oot o' the world wi' him.'

Officials, fearing that further delay would have disastrous consequences, ordered the hangman to do his business. As he drew the white cap over the murderer's face Mair called out: "Let them be clothed in shame! I curse them a'. . .a'. . .a'. . ."

Then the bolt was drawn and Allan Mair was hanging by the neck.

But seconds later the cheering crowd was stung into silence when the hanged man raised his hand to the back of his neck. He seized the rope and tried to get free. The people cried: "Good God! he's burst his bands asunder and means to save himself.'

The hangman pulled Mair's hand away and then grabbed his legs giving them a short tug.

As a chronicler of the day put it: "Amidst a gutteral sound from his lips, and a yell from the excited crowd, Allan Mair's head fell to the side, and he was dead."

This was the last public execution in Stirling.